Piety and the Princeton Theologians

Archibald Alexander, Charles Hodge, and Benjamin Warfield

By W. Andrew Hoffecker

BAKER BOOK HOUSE
Grand Rapids, Michigan

Printed in the United States of America

ISBN: 0-8010-4253-4

CONTENTS

ACKNOWLEDGMENTS

Portions of this study were previously published in slightly altered form in the festschrift for Dr. John Gerstner, *Soli Deo Gloria,* Presbyterian and Reformed Publishing Company, 1976 and in "The Devotional Life of Archibald Alexander, Charles Hodge, and Benjamin B. Warfield," *Westminster Theological Journal,* 42, no. 1, 1979.

I would like to acknowledge several who have enabled me to complete this study with a relative lack of difficulty. Staff members of Speer Library at Princeton Theological Seminary were very helpful in giving me access to manuscript collections of sermons and personal writings of Alexander, Hodge, and Warfield. Mrs. Mary Mattocks worked diligently typing the manuscript. She was as efficient as she was pleasant and encouraging in her comments while typing and awaiting news from the publisher.

Finally, as is so often recorded in "acknowledgments," I thank my wife. Few have epitomized genuine piety to me as she has since we met almost 20 years ago. While my efforts in teaching have been intended to exemplify a theology of the intellect, her witness in word and life has brought a theology of the heart into the soul of our marriage.

INTRODUCTION

Princeton theology was an attempt to maintain Calvinist theology and experience in America during the nineteenth and the opening decades of the twentieth centuries. Within the Princeton theology the subject of religious experience was as integral a part as any discussion of strictly doctrinal issues. In such writings as Archibald Alexander's *Thoughts on Religious Experience*, Charles Hodge's *The Way of Life*, and Benjamin B. Warfield's *Calvin and Augustine* are sufficient references to experiential faith to substantiate the Princeton theologians' concern for both doctrine and piety. Because they constantly related experience to doctrine, they composed a theology of religious experience that is as important for understanding the Princeton theology as any other of their writings on theological topics.

Unfortunately, scholars of American theology and church history have neglected the Princeton piety. Statements have been made to the effect that personal piety was intense among Princeton theologians but that it made little impact upon an otherwise intellectualistic treatment of the Christian faith. The resulting impression has been that not only was the subject of religious experience eclipsed by their stress on doctrine, but that Alexander, Hodge, and Warfield effected an artificial compartmentalization of their own experience and beliefs. This study represents in part an attempt to correct this misconception and to bring to a focus the important role that the discussion of Christian experience played in their theologies. Their intention was to maintain a balance between the intellectual and affective elements in the Christian faith.

In order to exhibit this balance I will consider each man with regard to his own religious experience, his writings of a more systematic nature on the subject of religious experience, and his writings of a more devotional nature. In consideration of the first point, biographies, diaries, and journals that exist will be examined. Unfortunately, one of the characteristics the Princeton men had in common was a reticence to talk about their personal religious experiences. This notwithstanding, the biographies of Alexander and Hodge and the short diaries and journals which have been preserved provide invaluable material on this aspect of their lives. The situation is different with Warfield. To my knowledge no biography exists, and no diaries or journals remain from his pen. Nevertheless, as in the case of Alexander and Hodge, some testimonies exist from outside sources which witness to the general character of Warfield's experience, and such material will be adduced. It is unfortunate that such a relatively large gap exists in our knowledge of Warfield, and this misfortune is compounded when the character of this missing information is considered.

The second area I will consider is the systematic writings of these men. The subjects which will be examined from these writings are discussions of doctrinal issues such as the nature of faith, the use of the Scriptures, the kinds of evidence for Christian faith, and the work of the Holy Spirit.

While Hodge was the only one to publish a systematic theology, two considerations should be kept in mind. The first is that Hodge and Alexander had such an intimate association that this intimacy extended to the area of theological matters, so much so that they were in virtual agreement in almost all matters. Alexander died before the publishing of Hodge's *magnum opus*, but had he been living he would have probably concurred with Hodge's opinions. The second is that Warfield never published his own systematic theology, which is a tacit admission that Hodge's work was satisfactory. This is not to say that no differences existed between these men, but rather that a remarkable consensus was manifest.

As the systematic or more formal works are examined it becomes evident that the Princeton theology of religious experience is a result of reactions to two approaches which erred in opposite directions. The first approach erred in stressing only the role that the cognitive powers play in the act of faith. Such an approach was characteristic of the deists, the speculative philosophers, the Roman Catholic Church, and some Presbyterians as well. In each case assent to propositions is of primary importance with no corresponding emphasis on the subjective state of the believing individual. The other approach emphasized the subjective state of the believer to the depreciation of the objective content of what is believed and the corresponding role that the mind plays in apprehending them. The figures that loomed large in this approach were the revivalists, the German theologian Friedrich Schleiermacher, the Quakers, and certain mystics. The Princeton men usually reduced the thought of these figures to the primacy of feeling whether it be the emotional phenomena of the revivalists, Schleiermacher's feeling of dependence, or the Quakers' and mystics' stress on the sensed immediate work of the Holy Spirit on the soul.

The Princeton men considered their task to be that of forging a *via media* between the two. While a *via media* represents the goal sought by the Princeton men so that both the objective content of the Scriptures and doctrine and the believer's subjective state are emphasized, it soon becomes apparent which of the two errors in method is considered more dangerous. Whereas the threat to Christianity was at one time that of the deists and speculative philosophers, the greater threat to the nineteenth-century theological scene appeared to be that of subjectivism. Nevertheless, Princeton men did not, therefore, neglect the subjective aspect but based it instead on the objective facts of the Christian faith which God had revealed.

The third consideration in each chapter will be the devotional writings of these men. Tracts, sermons, and conference addresses represent a somewhat neglected aspect of the Princeton theology. However, according to some reports it was the weekly conferences held in the seminary oratory on matters of practical religion that provided the greatest impact that these men had on their students. Such subjects as faith, contemplation of the Scriptures, the work of the Holy Spirit, and communion with God were stressed as the primary elements of practical faith. In this third section these subjects will receive primary attention with reference made to the first two sections of each chapter to integrate the results of each investigation. What emerges is that these men had as strong a concern for the nature of religious experience as they did for the soundness of Christian doctrine. They had a clearly established priority, however, and were careful that the touchstone for both matters be the Scriptures. Nevertheless, instances will be noted when this priority was reversed in practice, indicating that their statements on experience were not insignificant appendices to doctrine.

A final historical note should be made in this introduction. Since this is a study in historical theology, I would remind the reader that even though Alexander, Hodge, and Warfield expressed a unanimity of opinion on religious experience, they did not confront common theological and historical environments. In the 100 years between 1812 when Alexander assumed his professorship and 1912 when Warfield died, historical and theological contexts underwent profound changes.

Alexander and Hodge participated in the Old School—New School debate among Presbyterians which resulted in schism in 1837. While considering themselves a mediating element between two factions, they actually supported Old School views on all matters of doctrine and polity at issue. Alexander and Hodge actively fought for Calvinism even though it was beginning to decline as a major intellectual force in American culture. Hodge, for example, wrote many articles opposing New Haven Theology and its practical application in Charles Finney's "new measures."

In the latter years of his tenure Hodge faced not simply Arminianism's inroads but also higher and lower criticism. He actually contributed to fundamentalism's origin with his staunch defense of biblical authority. Warfield continued Hodge's views by defending Scripture from liberal attacks. However, while Warfield considered Calvinism as a viable theological option, most American thinkers had not only adopted Arminian principles but had accepted critical theories as well. Warfield's perception of conflicting liberal and conservative opinions is mirrored in his preoccupation with apologetics as a full-blown preparatory theological discipline.

Therefore, two widely different historical contexts characterize the milieu in which Princeton theology had its heyday. Such differences are to be remembered in light of our major emphasis that all three men advocated quite similar ideas on religious experience.

CHAPTER ONE

ARCHIBALD ALEXANDER: PRINCETON PASTOR

Archibald Alexander delivered a farewell sermon to his Philadelphia congregation on the occasion of his departure to become the first professor at Princeton Seminary in 1812. His text was Acts 20:26, 27, which in part contained the apostle Paul's claim that he had not failed to preach the whole counsel of God. Alexander slightly enlarged that statement as he declared, "Two things I have constantly aimed at, first to inform the understanding, secondly to impress the heart."[1] Thus he summed up what could easily stand as the motto for his career as missionary, pastor, and theological professor. His activity in missionary travels in Virginia and North Carolina in the closing decade of the eighteenth century, his pastorate in the Pine Street Church in Philadelphia from 1807–1812, and his 39 years as a professor at Princeton Seminary demonstrate his overriding concern for the relation between Christian teaching and Christian experience. It was altogether fitting that he become the first professor at Princeton, for one of its guiding principles was that a seminary be a "nursery of vital piety as well as of sound theological learning. . . ."[2] Alexander began a tradition at Princeton which resulted in an easily identifiable "Princeton piety." Frederick Wm. Loetscher contended that Alexander "put the stamp of his scholarly attainments and his fervent piety upon the whole life of the seminary."[3] His son, Lefferts A. Loetscher, likewise asserted that "in Dr. Alexander is to be found, in germ, the entire Princeton Theology."[4]

Other studies have demonstrated the development of the Princeton theology and Alexander's role in this development.[5] My task is to delineate in detail the Christian experience advocated by Alexander and the relation between the objective and subjective elements in that experience. None of the other Princeton men showed a greater preoccupation with the subject of religious experience than Archibald Alexander. Three of his many published

---

1. "Farewell Sermon . . . upon Leaving Philadelphia for Princeton" (n.p.).
2. *Life of Archibald Alexander*, p. 326, hereafter noted *LAA*.
3. *Dictionary of American Biography*, 1: 163.
4. *The Broadening Church*, p. 23.
5. Cf. John Oliver Nelson, "The Rise of the Princeton Theology," unpublished Ph.D. thesis (Yale, 1935), hereafter "Rise"; Lefferts A. Loetscher, *The Broadening Church*.

works—*Thoughts on Religious Experience* (1844), *Practical Sermons to be Read in Families and Social Meetings* (1850), and *Practical Truths* (1851) —establish him as the "pastor" of Princeton. It was not that he lacked Charles Hodge's theological ability or the apologetic interest of Benjamin B. Warfield. After all, Alexander's position as first professor in the seminary required that he teach both didactic and polemical theology, which are roughly equivalent to systematic theology and apologetics. Nevertheless, Alexander's preoccupation with religious experience marks him as preeminently a pastor.

Alexander's Personal Religious Life

Alexander did not always have this interest in religious experience. He was reared among Presbyterians who looked disparagingly upon conversion experiences. As a young person he remembered being temporarily affected by a travelling preacher. This impression was only temporary as his parents deprecated the man's message, and the rest of the people of Lexington, Virginia, shared an aversion to religion and the few religious people in the area. Although he rarely heard of conversions among the Presbyterians, and experiences of this type were subjects of ridicule, he did receive religious instruction. He learned the Shorter Catechism and portions of the Larger. Nevertheless, he reminisced that his childhood religious condition was one of virtual ignorance.[6] By his own confession he was generally uninterested in spiritual things even though he attended worship regularly.

> I did not delight to hear of God and his government, of his perfect law and the sad consequences of violating his precepts and what seems, at first sight, more strange, I had as little pleasure in hearing of Christ and his wonderful work of redemption. Even the idea of heaven itself afforded me no delight. . . . The reason why all religious subjects were distasteful was . . . that the idea of *sanctity* was connected with them all, and with none more than with the truths which related to Christ and to heaven.[7]

It was while he served as a tutor at the age of 17 in the home of General John Posey that Alexander's experience widened considerably. Mrs. Tyler,

---

6. *LAA*, pp. 32, 33, 36.
7. *Sermons*, "Sincere Soul's inquiry into Its Own State" (n.p.). All of Alexander's and Hodge's sermon manuscripts contain a shorthand made necessary by their length, which often was nearly 50 pages. Abbreviations and other shorthand notations have been written out so that they might be readily understood.

an elderly Baptist lady who lived with the Poseys, took a special interest in him and his spiritual welfare. Her comment on the Presbyterians was that while they exhibited all the traits of doctrinal soundness, they were singularly deficient in the area of experience. At her request he attended the local Baptist church, where he witnessed an example of the enthusiasm which he was later to criticize so sharply.[8] He had a conversation with a Baptist minister subsequent to his visit to the church which left him strangely puzzled as it concerned the "new birth," a subject he had never heard discussed among the Presbyterians.[9] Also while at the Posey home he read a book on the *Internal Evidences of the Christian Religion* by Soame Jenyns which produced a profound impression upon him.

> At every step conviction flashed across my mind, with such bright and overwhelming evidence, that when I ceased to read, the room had the appearance of being illuminated. I never had such a feeling from the simple discovery of truth. And it is my opinion, that no argument of the external or historical kind would have produced such a conviction.[10]

So much was his interest aroused in experiencing salvation that he began to retire to a place in the woods for times of prayer. Even though these times were delightful to him, they were not accompanied by the radical change he expected in his character.

When Alexander returned to Lexington he found that revival had come to the valley in which he lived. This was a new phenomenon for the Scotch Presbyterians. Conversion was virtually an unknown experience to them. It was the consensus of the inhabitants that despite reports of the revival's success in western Pennsylvania such religious commotions were little more than passing fancies. This was decidedly not the case with the young Alexander, whose interest in religious experience had been so stirred during his absence from Lexington.

The young seeker continued to have seasons of devotions in secret. On one occasion he was overcome "with such a melting of heart as I never had before or since . . . my eyes became a fountain of tears. . . . When I now reflect upon it, it seems like a sudden change in the animal system. . . ."[11] Such periods of emotional joy bordering on ecstasy were relentlessly followed by even deeper feelings of despair and hopelessness

---

8. *LAA*, p. 39.
9. Ibid., p. 41.
10. Ibid., p. 43.
11. Ibid., p. 62.

resulting from no permanent change in his character. He began to feel that he had enjoyed the best of opportunities yet without effect. He confessed having no better thoughts toward God but acquiesced in his just condemnation. He could only approve that his sentence to hell would be entirely just. However, upon wise spiritual counsel from a pastor his views changed still another time when he was told that no greater conviction was necessary. All that was needful was a view that Christ was his advocate. Alexander describes this new possibility of salvation as like a dawn after a dark night.[12]

After still more times of turbulent experiences Alexander determined to engage in prayer until he experienced salvation. This determination resulted in the following experience which is reported at length because of its significance for his later writings.

> I prayed, and then read in the Bible, prayed and read, prayed and read, until my strength was exhausted. . . . But the more I strove the harder my heart became, and the more barren was my mind of every serious or tender feeling. . . . I was about to desist from the endeavor, when the thought occurred to me, that though I was helpless, and my case was nearly desperate, yet it would be well to cry to God to help me in this extremity. I knelt upon the ground, and had poured out perhaps a single petition . . . when, in a moment, I had such a view of a crucified Savior, as is without parallel in my experience. The whole plan of grace appeared as clear as day. I was persuaded that God was willing to accept me, just as I was, and convinced that I had never before understood the freeness of salvation, but had always been striving to bring some price in my hand, or to prepare myself for receiving Christ. Now I discovered that I could receive him in all his offices at that very moment. . . . I felt truly a joy which was unspeakable and full of glory.[13]

Alexander then reports that he opened his Bible to passages in the book of John. The sacred page seemed "illuminated" to him. But more importantly, ". . . the truths were new, as if I had never read them before; and I thought it would be always thus."[14] For the first time he felt the freedom to undertake a written covenant with God, having previously considered this action but never feeling free to do so. He proceeded to record ("exactly from my feeling") this covenant. Alexander decided to make purification the test of his experience as he had done before. He had no doubts as to his sincerity

12. Ibid., p. 64.
13. Ibid., p. 70.
14. Ibid., pp. 70, 71.

of faith and considered the written covenant evidence of his having indeed received Christ during that experience if at no other time previously. Serenity marked his experience for a short time, but a week had not passed until corruption and darkness came upon him again. He made a confession of faith in 1789 but was without comfort upon his first experience at the Lord's Table. He feared that he might eat and drink damnation to himself.[15] His second communion, however, was accompanied with feelings of assurance in his salvation. That even after an experience which included clear views of Christ and an apprehension of the truths of Christianity one should still experience doubt and discouragement led Alexander to conclude that it was often impossible for one to know precisely when he had experienced regeneration. Thus at the time of his fluctuation between periods of joy and despair he was sure that it was during the Lexington revival in 1789 that he experienced salvation. However, looking back over his experience at the age of 77, he dated his new birth during his stay with the Posey family in 1788.

It was not usual for Alexander to talk about his religious experience. Both his son and Charles Hodge, his successor, refer to his general reticence to discuss his personal religious life. His son said that he was the most silent of anyone he ever knew in these matters.[16] Hodge, in a memorial to Alexander in the *Biblical Repertory,* underscored this point.

> He seldom spoke of his own experience or of his methods of religious culture. He lived with God: and men knew that he had been on the mount by the shining on his face; but he was not wont to tell what he saw, and he made no record.[17]

While this is true in general, a copy of a religious journal kept in 1791–92 has survived.

The journal is remarkable because of the profuse references to fears that he had fallen into apostasy. It reads like a hospital graph of his spiritual health from October 1791–July 1792. It is a recollection of his spiritual feelings, principally on occasions when he either preached in public or participated in leading public worship, and of his own private religious life. According to Alexander's son this practice was a direct effect of the revivals, in that it was the practice of revivalists to take new converts and put them on display, as it were, as possessing gifts of fluency in public testimonies and

---

15. Reference to Paul's statement in I Cor. 11.
16. *LAA,* p. 694.
17. "Memoir of Dr. Alexander," *Biblical Repertory and Princeton Review,* 27, no. 1: 151.

prayers evidencing their conversions.[18] Alexander's journal bears this out. In the entry for October 16 Alexander states, "In my first prayer I had composure . . . though not much affection . . . had considerable sweetness in secret prayer in the evening."[19] Alexander's public experiences fluctuated between instances of "keen anguish of spirit" in which he found it very difficult to pray or give testimony and other times of which he wrote, "my heart was enlarged, my feelings were lively, so that I found delight in the utterance of truth." During the latter his train of thought, although unpremeditated, was fluent and his words apparently well received.[20] Most of the journal, however, is devoted to his own spiritual progress, or more often, the lack of it, in his experience. The most despairing of all the entries was for March 23, 1792, in which he confesses that in the three years since his conversion he had not remembered being in a more "stupid, insensible state." Indeed he felt bereft of any "heart to perform any of the duties of religion."[21]

The journal is not without entries of a more positive nature. Some give the impression of great joyfulness. Thus the record for August 30, 1792: "O! How sweet are the exercises of religion when God is present. Where the Spirit of God is, there is liberty indeed."[22] In some of these accounts mention is made only of his feelings without any reference to their cause such as those which simply state how Alexander felt upon arising each morning from bed. In other instances, an explicit connection is drawn between the remembrance of specific Scripture verses and the subsequent change in the subject's religious feelings. The latter was to form the very heart of his thinking on religious experience.

The keeping of such diaries was later discouraged by Alexander in his criticisms of revivalism. Alexander's journal was a function of his participation in the revival. New converts were encouraged to speak in public, and with so much attention given to the state of one's religious feelings, pathological introspection often developed as Alexander's journal illustrates. These entries are the result of his senstive conscience and of an attempt to keep careful track of his feelings. However, the practice of a proper, even intense, spiritual introspection was to be a continuing emphasis not only in

---

18. Ibid., p. 76.
19. "Journal Oct. 1 - Dec. 31, 1791" (n.p.), hereafter "Journal."
20. *LAA*, p. 86.
21. Ibid.
22. Ibid.

Alexander's thought but also in the other Princeton men's writings. Not only had religious experience become a matter of concern, it had become a prominent element to be carefully scrutinized, nourished, and guarded. This was no more forcefully illustrated than by the devotional life which Alexander attempted to maintain. At first it consisted of reading the Scriptures and other literature and prayer. Later Alexander made repeated use of the Bible in the original Hebrew and Greek. He used a Hebrew Psalter given to him by Charles Hodge to chant the Psalms. He was often known to seclude himself completely for a day of abstinence. His son reports that he gave evidences of great assurance of his faith despite earlier struggles and that he placed the highest premium on "personal communion with the Lord Jesus Christ, as the very heart of religion and happiness. On this subject, his sentiments often arose to a blissful rapture. . . ."[23]

Religious experience was a recurring subject in his personal correspondence. On some occasions Alexander simply summarized the general state of religion where he was located:

> . . . there is much less religious knowledge among the bulk of the people here than in the country. Multitudes grow up with very little knowledge of the doctrines of religion, and many after they are grown join themselves to a congregation by taking pews, who were never instructed at all.[24]

> We have had a precious shower of grace here, without any new measures, or any undue excitement.[25] Religion in this place is at present in a languid rather than a thriving state. . . .[26]

When Charles Hodge travelled to Europe to study in 1827–28, Alexander was very concerned for Hodge's spiritual life, that he not be shaken in his orthodox beliefs. He counselled young Hodge, with whom he shared a strong personal attachment, to beware of thinking that is opposed to orthodoxy.

> I hope while you are separated from your earthly friends, you will take care to keep the communication with heaven open! Remember that you breathe a poisoned atmosphere. If you lose the lively and deep impression of divine truth—if you fall into skepticism or even into coldness,

---

23. Ibid., pp. 694-95.
24. Ibid., p. 283.
25. Ibid., p. 547. Note reference to "new measures"; cf. below.
26. Ibid., p. 285. Cf. collection of "Letters to Charles Hodge," which were written to Hodge while he was in Germany. Some of Alexander's letters read like revival meeting statistics as he mentions meetings in Trenton, New York, and among the students at Princeton.

you will lose more than you gain from all the German professors and libraries.[27]

There is a twofold emphasis here: that Hodge maintain his orthodox views and that his spirituality be maintained. The same emphasis on doctrine and piety is reflected in a subsequent letter dated August 16, 1827: "I hope and pray that you may not lose any thing of the love of the truth and spirituality of mind."[28]

Thus we have a rather detailed view of Alexander's religious life drawn not only from secondary accounts but also from personal recollections and correspondence. These sources reveal a continuing personal concern for the experiential element in religion from his own conversion experience to the general practice of piety. Of great significance is the prominent influence that revivalism had on his life. Although he was to have some critical words for revivalism in his late writings, to be dealt with below, the revival of 1789 received his general approbation. The positive approach to revival conversion experiences which he retained in varying degrees is due in part to the fact that his first encounter with revivals was a positive one. The negative comments that he had for the emotional excesses and doctrinal deviations of other revivals are not the observations of a detached critic. Rather they are the considered words of one who had experienced what he considered to be both good and bad religious experiences through his participation in the Lexington revival. The very fact that these were so varied enabled him to write with such understanding and perception on those which he criticized as well as those which he advocated. He was not to encourage one particular kind of experience because he lacked experiential acquaintance with others. The turbulent fluctuations of his emotions during his youth turned out to be a disguised blessing when it came time to criticize emotional excesses.

This account of Alexander's life is important also for the light it sheds on the Princeton piety. Not only did a direct relationship exist between Alexander's own experience and the position which he was to propound in his writings, but the lines were being drawn which were to serve as the basis of the experience which his successors were to advocate as well. One is struck by the abundant references to feelings and emotions in Alexander's account. The references are not only profuse in number but also seem to take the

---

27. A. A. Hodge, *Life of Charles Hodge*, p. 160.
28. Ibid., p. 161.

position of prominence in the narrative. Some narratives are notable for the references to his feelings which border on the ecstatic: tears, joy, sorrow, the "illuminated page," happiness, etc. What distinguished these experiences from that in which he engaged in a written covenant was the "view of a crucified Savior" and his perception of the "whole plan of grace . . . plain as day" in the latter. In fact his reception of Christ was in terms of "all his offices." This implies that the feelings of "joy . . . unspeakable and full of glory" had as their foundation an understanding which was more complete than ever before. Not that perception of truth did not precede the emotional experiences on other occasions. Nevertheless, the level of intellectual understanding was sufficient on this occasion to give him confidence enough to make a covenant with God.

This principle that experience was to be based on an intellectual apprehension of the objective truths of Christianity was to become a *sine qua non* in the Princeton piety. Experience which has no such basis is immediately suspect as a *Christian* experience. Without the foundation of specifically Christian doctrine, any experience that one has can only be attributed to either the mere emotional temperament of the person or the natural religious feelings which everyone has but which are not Christian in content.

Systematic Treatment of Religious Experience

Archibald Alexander wrote no systematic theology. However, he wrote extensively on various subjects ranging from biblical criticism to the area which this study treats. Therefore, it is necessary to turn to those writings of a more formal nature which were published either as monographs or articles in the *Princeton Review*. Before investigating these writings mention should be made of Alexander's theological and philosophical background. From the inception of Princeton Seminary until Hodge wrote his *Systematic Theology* in 1871–72, the theology text used was Francis Turretine's *Institutio Theologiae Elencticae*. Alexander's son acknowledged that this seventeenth-century work was "ponderous, scholastic and in a dead language." Nevertheless, he said his father considered the gains to be acquired by working through its 20 *loci* and their subdivided *questiones* fitted men to be "strong and logical divines."[29]

John Oliver Nelson in his analysis of Alexander's use of Turretine contends that Alexander actually "exorcized" Turretine—i.e., while he

---

29. Ibid., p. 386.

accepted the "broad principles" of his theology he viewed the "formal and legal refinements" as only "adiaphora" in all details. In fact in choosing Turretine he passed over the rationalist eighteenth century and the legalist seventeenth century in Britain to get to the systematic Calvinism of Geneva.[30]

Dr. Hodge testified to the use made of Turretine calling the *Institutio* one of the "most perspicuous books ever written." According to Hodge students were assigned from 20 to 40 quarto pages in Latin to be prepared for recitation. His lifelong friend, Bishop John Johns of the Episcopal Church, apparently excelled in class recitation.

> [He could recite] . . . the State of the Question, all the arguments in its support in their order, all objections and the answers to them, through . . . thirty or forty pages without the professor [sic] saying a word to him. This is what in the College of New Jersey used to be called rowling. Whatever may be thought of this method of instruction, it certainly was effective. A man who passed through that drill never got over it.[31]

As for the philosophical background of his thought, Alexander followed the lead of John Witherspoon, who advocated the Scottish common sense realism of Reid and Stewart. Witherspoon became president of the College of New Jersey in Princeton in 1768. This influence of the Scottish philosophy will become evident as the writings of all three Princeton men are examined. It accounts for certain rationalistic tendencies which tended to pervade their writings.[32] With this background in mind we shall turn to Alexander's published writings.

Alexander wrote a preface to Isaac Watt's *A Rational Defense of the Gospel* in which he contended that what distinguishes Watt's theological defenses is "the vein of evangelical piety which runs through them."[33] Although the admitted objective of the book is to meet the objections of skeptics and to refute error, Alexander asserted that it would concomitantly fulfil a pastoral objective as well.

---

30. Nelson explains Alexander's choice of Turretine and his use of the Genevan theologian's writings in "*Rise,*" pp. 268-73. Also cf. Ernest R. Sandeen, op. cit., p. 320, n. 32 in which he contends that later Princeton men were more influenced by Turretine when they were students than was Alexander who assigned Turretine's theology to them as a text.
31. "A Discourse delivered at the re-opening of the Chapel," p. 19
32. Alexander's role in the influx of Scottish common sense in American theology is treated by Sydney E. Ahlstrom in "The Scottish Philosophy and American Theology," *Church History*, 24 (1955): 257-72.
33. Watts, *A Rational Defense of the Gospel*, p. iii.

In my opinion, the work is calculated to be eminently useful . . . not only by removing doubts and objections which relate to the truth of Christianity, but also by unfolding the true nature of the plan of redemption, and by making a salutary impression on the heart.[34]

This juxtaposition of the intellectual and emotive needs is reminiscent of Alexander's stated intention as a pastor to inform the understanding and impress the heart. Alexander's method, whether preaching or teaching, always evidenced a conscious effort to meet both intellectual and emotional needs. Whether he was writing a treatise on the evidences of Christianity or preaching a sermon, the objective remained the same.

In the writings now under consideration that is borne out by an examination of the several works on evidences. His "A Brief Outline of the Evidences of the Christian Religion"[35] begins with an apologetic for the right use of reason in religion. The Scottish philosophy mentioned above is strongly evident as he contended that reason is indispensable in religion for without it one would be unable to evaluate properly the evidences for revelation, to interpret the revelation, or to give assent to its doctrines. Since religion is based on truth, no conception can be made without reason.

Truth and reason are so intimately connected, that they can never, with propriety, be separated. Truth is the object, and reason the faculty by which it is apprehended, whatever be the nature of the truth, or the evidence by which it is established. . . . In receiving, therefore, the most mysterious doctrines of revelation, the ultimate appeal is to reason.[36]

Alexander is careful, however, to limit the role of reason lest he advocate a full-blown rationalism. By limiting the role of reason Alexander intended to prevent Christian belief from degenerating into mere philosophical speculation. His opposition to philosophical speculation was the first of a two-front attack which he waged over the nature of religious experience. Although he argues against those who conclude that all religions are alike, and against those who have an impassioned prejudice against religion, the sharpest critique in the "Brief Outline" is directed against the "cold, speculative, subtle sect of skeptics who involve themselves in a thick mist of meta-

---

34. Ibid., p. v.
35. "A Brief Outline of the Evidences of the Christian Religion" was originally written as a sermon in 1823. Due to demand it was expanded for publication by the Princeton Press. Hereafter "A Brief Outline."
36. "A Brief Outline," pp. 6, 7.

physics, attack first principles, and confound their readers with paradoxes in their hands. . . . "[37]

The method of philosophical speculation predisposes those who use it away from the knowledge of the truth which in turn prohibits any valid religious experience. Such philosophers are guilty of several errors. They cunningly assume false principles as their starting point, and when they on rare occasions begin with valid principles they are guilty of sophistical misrepresentation. They often project their inquiries beyond the limits of human knowledge. This false dependence on human knowledge which fails to apprehend truth illustrates the necessity of divine revelation. A distinct difference obtains between the feeble working of reason and the distinct clarity of God's revelations.

> In reasoning about the most important truths, men differ exceedingly from one another: and this very circumstance spreads doubt and uncertainty over all their speculations. When we peruse the discourses of the wisest of heathen sages . . . [they] sometimes seemed to entertain a glimmering hope, that at some future period . . . divine instruction might be communicated. . . . [38]

Often he calls the motives of the philosophers into question asserting that their intention is to "pull down everything" and "erect nothing to replace it."[39]

In still another treatise Alexander contends that speculative faith differs from a living faith because speculation neither apprehends its object nor affects the individual. He likens speculative opinion to that of a dead faith. It is merely a matter of head knowledge, whereas living faith has an effect on the heart. "The one is seated in the heart and influences the will and affections in such a manner as to become a ruling principle of action, whereas the other only swims in the brain and produces no real effect upon the heart. . . ."[40] But of still greater importance is the fact that a speculative opinion never really apprehends its object. The differences between these two kinds of faith are no more strikingly apparent than when they are applied to Christ.

---

37. Ibid., pp. 10, 11. The second front he attacked was revivalist experience. It is treated below.

38. *Evidences of the Authenticity, Inspiration, and Canonical Authority of the Holy Scriptures*, p. 40, hereafter *Evidences*.

39. Ibid., p. 12.

40. "A Treatise in which the Difference between a Living and Dead Faith is Explained," p. 5, hereafter "Treatise." Cf. Calvin's remark that without piety knowledge of God "flits in the brain" (*Institutes of the Christian Religion*, I, v, 9).

. . . a living Faith always lays hold of and embraces its object; whereas a dead faith has no such property but rests in mere speculation. When Christ the special object of Faith is brought to the view of the soul a living Faith always appropriates him, chooses him as a Savior suitable to itself, receives him as its portion, trusts and depends upon him alone for salvation, resigns itself up to him alone to be governed and directed agreeable to his will, and is pleased and delighted with him above all things. . . . Faith is called committing oneself to the Lord . . . a dead Faith is not exercised towards him in any such manner.[41]

Alexander cites the deists as exemplifying speculative belief, for their beliefs failed to produce what he insisted true Christian belief did—piety or devotion. The question of whether there has ever been a "pious deist" is almost as ludicrous as asking whether there has ever been an honest thief or a sober drunkard. The two terms are simply antithetical. Alexander intended no ridicule toward the deists since they would have been the first to deny any pretense of devotion. In fact they would regard such terms as "pious" or "devout" as statements of ridicule.[42]

In Alexander's opinion this lack of concern for piety rendered the deists incapable of establishing and perpetuating a religious worship. Their speculative opinions by their very nature failed to produce an experiential element. The Theophilanthropists of France, who managed to receive support from the directory of France during the revolution, were a case in point. They had a creed of two articles, the existence of God and immortality of the soul. Their leaders devised worship services of prayer and praise in a manual, and planned lectures to popularize the society's goals. Alexander emphasizes the distinct advantages which the society enjoyed—government support, patronization by intellectuals, buildings donated by the state. However, the society failed, and Alexander posits as the prominent cause the absence of a devotional spirit. "There was nothing to interest the feelings of the heart."[43] One of the elements that brings men together in worship is the tendency for people of similar feelings to commune together. Their natural response to the being whom they worship will be that of praise, love, and adoration. The emotions of the heart cannot be smothered if true piety is to exist.

> Piety, it is true, consists essentially in the exercises of the heart; but that religion which is merely mental, is suspicious; at best very feeble; it is

41. "Treatise," pp. 7, 8.
42. *Evidences*, pp. 30, 31.
43. Ibid., p. 34.

not likely to produce any permanent effect on the character or comfort of the person entertaining it; and cannot be useful to others in the way of example.[44]

The most significant of Alexander's criticisms of speculative faith were levied against his own Presbyterian ancestors. Some people though obviously fully catechized never speak of their own religious experiences. No matter what reasons they have for not doing so, it is clear that whenever cases of religious experience are discussed, these people always "propose the case in the third person."

They will talk to you by the hour and the day, about the doctrines of religion and show that they are more conversant with their Bibles, than many who talk much of their religious feelings.[45]

That he should group these people with deists and philosophers is of striking importance. However, the divorce between theology and experience which such Christians created makes it very clear that their method "has the effect of keeping out of view the necessity of a change of heart."[46] Although Alexander does not elaborate this criticism and never specifically identifies those against whom he charges this serious error, the group that best fits his description are those Presbyterians who are thoroughly orthodox in their theology, having been schooled in the Westminster catechisms, and yet remain as deficient in experience as philosophers.

To be sure Alexander never proposed the elimination of oxthodox doctrine and knowledge of the Scripture as a corrective to Presbyterian deficiencies. Nevertheless he viewed such orthodoxy as mere dead faith if it is not accompanied with an experimental knowledge. Alexander's criticism of speculative, historical, or dead faith includes, therefore, several elements. The first is that it drives a wedge between man's intellectual and emotional faculties which must work in concert for valid religious experience. Speculative faith on the other hand is utterly destitute of any emotional element. Religious knowledge is only truly "religious" and "knowledge" in the fullest sense when the feelings and affections are excited. Only then do discernible acts of devotion and piety result.

This leads to a second criticism of speculative faith. The lack of acts of devotion and piety has both religious and ethical overtones which are closely interwoven. Speculative faith effects no moral transformation and produces

---

44. Ibid.
45. Ibid., p. 120-21.
46. Ibid., p. 121.

no religious acts of humility, praise, and love. Such absence is related in turn to a third deficiency in speculative faith. Christ is not truly apprehended at all. Since responses of pietistic devotion are not the goal of speculative knowledge, the individual has merely knowledge *about* Christ, which, in Alexander's view, is merely empty notions.[47]

Another emphasis in Alexander's works, which has been noticed in other studies, is the role of "evidences."[48] In his *Evidences,* chapters 6-12 outline the external evidences for the Scripture as authentic, inspired, and canonical. Prominent among them are miracles, the success of the gospel, and fulfillment of prophecy. Chapter 12 is a defense of the position that Christianity has the best kind of evidence for its Scriptures. However, in chapter 13 Alexander shifts to the internal evidences for the Scriptures. He notes that some have emphasized either the external or the internal to the exclusion of the other. He believes they supplement each other, neither being stressed to the exclusion of the other. However, in the end he feels that the internal are more effective in establishing the truth of the Scriptures.

> There is no propriety in disparaging one for the purpose of enhancing the value of the other. I believe, however, that more instances have occurred of skeptical men being convinced of the truth of Christianity by the internal than by the external evidences.[49]

What is necessary for the apprehension of the internal evidences is a "candid and docile disposition" unencumbered with antagonistic presuppositions as to the nature of the writings which raise "insuperable objections . . . at every step in the progress."[50] As for the nature of internal evidences of the Scriptures, a helpful analogy is to be found in the evidence for the being of God from the created world. The connecting link is the presupposition that everything which comes from God will unmistakably bear His impress.

> . . . every thing which proceeds from God . . . will contain and exhibit the impress of his character. As this is resplendently visible in

---

47. Saving faith as an experience is more fully treated below. The purpose for introducing it at this point is for comparison with speculative faith.

48. Cf. Loetscher, *The Broadening Church,* p. 22.

49. *Evidences,* p. 229. N.B., Alexander links the evidences for Christianity and the Scriptures and interchanges the two terms. Evidence for the one is evidence for the other. This exemplifies a continuing emphasis on the Scriptures, which the Princeton men stressed whether it be exegesis of its contents or defense of its inspiration etc. Cf. Ernest Sandeen, "The Princeton Theology," *Church History,* 31 (1962): 307-21.

50. *Evidences,* p. 230.

the heavens and in the earth, it is reasonable to think that it will not be less manifest in his word.[51]

What Alexander wants to avoid is the impression that the role of internal evidences can be transformed into a logical demonstration. Ordinary Christians have never depended on demonstrative arguments because these arguments presuppose vigorous argumentation which many are not able to follow. Christians, therefore, believe not on the basis of external evidence but on the basis of internal evidence "not indeed as perceived by the unaided intellect of man, but as it is exhibited to the mind by the illumination of the Holy Spirit."[52] He contends that if anyone will submit himself to reading the Scriptures without partiality, even the most skeptical will experience the efficacy of the internal evidences and will come under conviction of its divine origin and truth.

He describes the nature of internal evidence thus:

> It cannot easily be put into the form of logical argument, for it consists in moral fitness and beauty; in the adaptation of truth to the human mind; in its astonishing power of penetrating and searching the heart and affecting the conscience. There is a sublime sanctity in the doctrines and precepts of the gospel; a devotional and heavenly spirit pervading the Scriptures; a purity and holy tendency which cannot but be felt by the serious reader of the word of God; and a power to sooth and comfort the sorrowful mind. . . .[53]

Alexander continues for forty pages to describe the most prominent of the internal evidences. He concludes: "O PRECIOUS GOSPEL! Will any merciless hand endeavor to tear away from our hearts this best, this last, and sweetest consolation. . . ."[54]

John O. Nelson alleges that this strong emphasis on the subjective working of the internal evidences should be viewed as a concomitant of a thread of romanticism which runs throughout Alexander's life and writings.[55] Nelson contends that in his position on the subjective working of the internal evidences Alexander attributes to the "heavenliness of the matter itself" what the Westminster Confession predicates of the work of the Holy Spirit.

51. Ibid., p. 231-32.
52. Ibid., p. 232. It is noteworthy that Alexander's examination of the evidences omits any reference to what has been called the noetic effect of sin, that man's knowledge and ability to know was crippled by the fall. All three Princeton men omit any reference to the noetic effect of the fall.
53. Ibid., p. 233.
54. Ibid., p. 272.
55. "Rise," pp. 252-54.

Therefore, on this particular matter Alexander stands outside the tradition of the Westminster Confession. Nelson supports his contention by pointing out that the one and only reference made in the *Evidences* to the work of the Holy Spirit is the one quoted above. Rather than the Holy Spirit being the cause of the efficacy of the internal evidence. Nelson contends, "It was *he*, the exulting subject who saw divine power in the Scripture. To probe behind this romanticist immediacy to some objective services of the Spirit entailed a scholastic analysis which was unimportant. . . ."[56]

The inexplicable way in which internal evidence works on the mind, the heart, and the feelings is analogous, in Nelson's opinion, to the way in which scenes of nature affected the romantic Princeton professor. As an example he cites Alexander's recollection of the impression which the Natural Bridge of Rockbridge County, Virginia, made on him as a boy. Alexander confessed an inability to express the effect which the sight made on his mind. The juxtaposition of the natural arch against the sky, in Alexander's words, "produced an emotion entirely new; the feeling was as though something within sprung up to a great height by a kind of sudden impulse. That was the animal sensation which accompanied the genuine emotion of the sublime."[57]

When this romantic experience is seen to be analogous to the way in which a Christian perceives the internal evidences, Nelson contends that for Alexander no witness of the Holy Spirit is necessary. All men have this "innate religious faculty which leads them to recognize God's sovereignty."[58] So central is this "mystical immediacy that *there* is the direct agency of another spirit on our own," that Alexander builds his whole system of theology around this "intuitional apprehension of the absoluteness of Scripture."[59]

Nelson's analysis of Alexander's use of internal evidence as a function of his romantic tendencies helps us to understand how internal evidences affect the perceiving subject. This thread of romanticism is perceptible not only in Alexander's works but in Hodge's works as well and is developed most elaborately in Hodge's concept of beauty which we will note below. But Nelson, in rightly emphasizing romantic intuition as characterizing the believer's perception of the Scripture's heavenly content, is incorrect when

---

56. Ibid., p. 252.
57. *LAA*, pp. 29, 30. Other references to Alexander's appreciation of scenic beauty are found in the same section, pp. 24-31.
58. Nelson, op. cit., p. 254. Cf. Alexander's *Outlines of Moral Science*, p. 86: "The great Creator has not left himself without a witness in the breast of every man."
59. Ibid., p. 253.

he states that this perception is so immediate that the Holy Spirit's role in the generation of faith is thereby eliminated. Alexander included both intuition of internal evidences and the work of the Spirit despite Nelson's disclaimer. The precedent for including both the role of internal evidences and the role of the Spirit in Christian faith was the Westminster Confession, to which Nelson referred. The two elements are included in the first section on the Holy Scripture:

> We may be moved and induced by the testimony of the church to an high and reverent esteem for the Holy Scripture; and the heavenliness of the matter, the efficacy of the doctrine, the majesty of the style, the consent of all the parts, the scope of the whole (which is to give all glory to God) . . . the many other comparable excellencies, and the entire perfection thereof, are arguments whereby it doth abundantly evidence itself to be the word of God; yet, notwithstanding, our full persuasion and assurance of the infallible truth and divine authority thereof, is from the inward work of the Holy Spirit, bearing witness by and with the word in our hearts.[60]

Alexander retained this dual emphasis of the Westminster Confession in his writings. The work of the Spirit receives the most prominent emphasis in the rest of his writings, as we will note. But just as the Westminster Confession allows the internal evidence a significant place which does not preclude the witness of the Spirit as the ultimate factor in perceiving the truth of the Scriptures, so Alexander in his *Evidences* exults in the intuition which the believer has of the Scripture's divinity. Because the subject of the book is the evidences, we should expect Alexander to stress those evidences and their effects on the believer and not necessarily the role of the Holy Spirit. But the *Evidences* does not represent the totality of Alexander's thought.

For a balanced view of Alexander's position we must examine his clearest statement on the work of the Holy Spirit in an article "Practical View of Regeneration."

> The Spirit operates by and through the word. The word derives all its power and penetrating energy from the Spirit. . . . Men, it is true, are rational and accountable agents, and are therefore proper subjects of commands and exhortations; yet are they destitute of spiritual life, and no power but that of God . . . can communicate life. When the Spirit operates by the word, the soul before dead in sin is rendered susceptible of impression from divine truth. The entrance of the truth under this

---

60. *A Harmony of the Westminster Presbyterian Standards*, p. 17.

divine influence gives light, and excites holy affections, which prompt to good purposes. . . .[61]

The role of the Holy Spirit is to accompany the word with power to remove the spiritual blindness man experiences previous to regeneration. So central to Alexander's thinking was the illumination of the Holy Spirit that he devoted a part of his inaugural address at Princeton to it. As a challenge to the students he indicated that without the assistance of the Holy Spirit their search for truth would be futile. Especially in time of doubt is the Spirit necessary.

> . . . at many such times [of doubt] a lively impression made by the Spirit of truth, banishes all doubt and hesitation. . . . This may appear to some to savour of enthusiasm. Be it so. It is, however, an enthusiasm essential to the very nature of our holy religion, without which it would be a mere dry system of speculation, of ethics and ceremonies. But this divine illumination is its *life,* its *soul,* its essence.[62]

Therefore, not only was illumination of the Spirit necessary for conversion, it was requisite for the Christian life as well. Indeed not only are theological students in need of this anointing but every Christian must partake of it.

Therefore, Alexander's including both external and internal evidences in his theological thinking was consonant with the rest of his thought in which he made a conscious effort to maintain a balance between the objective and the subjective, the head and the heart, the intellect and the emotional. It almost appears as if a theological symmetry is the goal in his thinking. At times the intellectual element predominates and reason is stressed. At other times the subjective receives greater attention.

Nowhere did Alexander seek this balance with more determination than in his writings on Christian experience instigated by revivalism. Nelson outlines the history of this interest.[63] The salient factor was that the revivalism

---

61. *Biblical and Theological Review,* 8, no. 4 (1836): 482.

62. "Inaugural Address," p. 92 (emphasis his). Beginning with Alexander the Princeton men associated "enthusiasm" not only with revivalistic excess but also with claims of immediate inspiration of the Holy Spirit by dreams, visions, or immediate suggestions to the mind. Hodge developed this more fully in his thought. But Alexander wrote "Enthusiasm and Fanaticism" tracing a history of groups who taught the continued inspiration of the Holy Spirit from the Montanists to the Quakers. It was the latter group with their teaching that a light is given to all men sufficient to lead them in religious matters and that this light is the Holy Spirit that Princeton men opposed. They proposed that the proper work of the Holy Spirit is "illumination" and not "inspiration," which was reserved solely for the writers of Scriptures.

63. "Rise," pp. 225-64.

which affected the Presbyterian church in the 1800's was different from the revivalism of Whitefield and Tennent. Its impact on the church was considerable as the number of churches grew from 449 to 772 during the first decade of the nineteenth century. Princeton Seminary was founded in part to educate ministers for this growing church. The most significant difference from the earlier revivalism was the doctrine which was advocated. Especially controversial was the doctrine of God's sovereignty. With the growing lack of attention to this doctrine, conversion became less an experience of the "sheer cataclysmic power of God" as formerly under Whitefield and Tennent, and became more of a " 'religious experience' with no absolute realization of the truth involved."[64]

Thus many of the converts of the revival did not profess Calvinism. It fell to Alexander, who had been so profoundly affected in his youth by the revival himself, to attempt a rapprochement between those who advocated revival experience and those who stressed Reformed doctrine. Nelson states that the task was to forge a *via media* between the Scylla of mere doctrine and the Charybdis of mere animal commotion. This would be no easy task, but appropriately it was Alexander who exemplified doctrinal purity and evangelical fervor. His writings on religious experience must be seen against this background of division within the Presbyterians as to the nature of religious experience and the relation between doctrine and experience. At all points Alexander's objective was to be true to Calvinist doctrine while stressing the place of experience as well.

Alexander's strongest protest was against what he and other Presbyterians thought were the emotional excesses of the revivals such as "the jerks," violent physical behavior supposedly the manifestation of the Spirit's convicting power. He opposed these phenomena primarily because they were not reliable indications of the work of the Holy Spirit. If such phenomena are taken alone as the manifestation of the Spirit's working, they can be misleading, since other religions report instances of great emotional excitement. They have been common among "pagans, Mohammedans, heretics and Papists."[65]

This guilt by association was a prominent argument in Alexander's criticism of revivalistic enthusiasm. Alexander was in a dilemma when it

---

64. Ibid., p. 246.
65. "Letter 1," in Sprague's *Lectures on Revivals,* hereafter "Letter." Cf. "Enthusiasm and Fanaticism" and "Enthusiasm" in "Dr. Alexander's Sermons, Nov. 7, 1816 - Sept. 26, 1819," and *LAA*, p. 274.

came to the word "enthusiasm." In one sense he approved of it, specifying that every Christian who "feels the influence of the Holy Spirit may be called an enthusiast."[66] Alexander pointed out, however, that many groups who have opposed important doctrines such as the divinity of Christ and the atonement have reported an emotional excitement that could not have resulted from God's Spirit. Oftentimes the emotional state of the individual regarding religious matters is only a function of his own temperament and is in no way connected with the Holy Spirit. While some people are by temperament happy and enthusiastic, others are more susceptible to periods of melancholia. The mere presence of a particular emotional state, therefore, is not necessarily indicative of an individual's religious condition. Emotional excitement may be the result of mere natural religious feelings or the product of a person's normal emotional temperament. Particularly suspicious as a sign of true piety is the presence of spiritual melancholy, which in Alexander's opinion borders on insanity.[67]

Secondly, religious excitement is particularly susceptible to the dangers of mass suggestion or sympathy. Frequently in periods of excitement only a few are truly affected by the working of the Holy Spirit while the remainder of the people are merely in a state of sympathy with the former. Man's social nature makes him susceptible to such influences. Mass suggestion covers such diverse manifestations as yawning and coughing in a group to agitation of religious emotions.

> The wilder and stronger the passions which agitate others, the more are we affected by them. This operation of mutual sympathetic excitement, when many persons are brought together under some agitating influence, produces a stream of emotion which cannot easily be resisted; and far above what any one of the crowd would have felt, if the same cause had operated on him alone.[68]

Alexander calls special attention to that bodily agitation called "the jerks." It was well known, he stated, that this phenomenon and its variations were imported from other sections of the country and that its widespread occur-

66. "Dr. Alexander's Sermons," p. 29.
67. *Thoughts on Religious Experience*, p. 66. Alexander's "Journal" entry for Dec. 2, 1791, contains an example of melancholy. He reports visiting a lady who was "tormented with the most dreadful apprehensions, and such imaginations as are sufficient to affrighten every lady who sees her. She imagines that she is full of devils, and breathes flames continually out of her mouth. She thinks the house is continually beset with infernal powers. . . ."
68. Ibid., p. 70.

rence at meetings was "commonly produced by the sight of other persons thus affected; and if, in some instances, without the sight, yet by having the imagination impressed by hearing of such things."[69]

Alexander related a personal experience illustrating the principle of sympathy. He once attended a meeting in an unfamiliar territory. While seated at the fringe of the audience, he noticed that, as the preacher became more emotional in his preaching, a commotion began in the center of the room. A lady's voice pierced the air. Emotional excitement spread through the congregation, and Alexander confessed that he restrained himself from expressing his feelings only with great effort. But what was of particular interest to him was that a group of tobacco planters who sat near him talked throughout the service until the preacher began exhorting the people. Whereupon they joined in the agitation, having heard nothing of the message. He concluded that the feeling was communicated "by the mere sounds that were uttered; for many of the audience had not paid any attention to what was said; but nearly all partook of the agitation."[70]

However, Alexander, though disparaging sympathy when emotional excesses were its subject, was not totally opposed to the principle itself. His own religious disposition was too open to the place of religious emotions for him to deprecate mass sympathy *in toto*. He only opposed its abuse for "without it, how dull and uninteresting would social worship be."[71] Sympathy is a great blessing to those engaged in singing, praying, listening, or receiving the sacrament. When believers are thus gathered,

> . . . they form, as it were, one body, and the whole mass is melted down and amalgamated into one grand emotion. They seem to have but one heart and one soul, and harmoniously as their voices mingle in the sacred song of praise to the Redeemer, do their feelings amalgamate in one ascending volume, towards heaven.[72]

It is clear, therefore, that he disparaged sympathy only when it resulted in certain manifestations which did not accord with how he thought public worship should be conducted. When a genuine revival takes place, the emotional impact is deeply felt but has other manifestations: "There is not only no wildness and extravagance, but very little strong commotion of the animal feelings."[73]

---

69. Ibid.
70. Ibid., p. 78
71. Ibid., p. 71.
72. Ibid.
73. "Letter," p. 4.

> In such revivals there is great solemnity and silence. The convictions of sin are deep and humbling: the justice of God in the condemnation of the sinner is felt and acknowledged; every other refuge but Christ is abandoned; the heart at first is made to feel its own impenetrable hardness; but when least expected, it dissolves under a grateful sense of God's goodness and Christ's love; light breaks in upon the soul either by a gradual dawning, or by a sudden flash; Christ is revealed through the gospel, and a firm and often a joyful confidence of salvation through Him is produced; a benevolent, forgiving, meek, humble and contrite spirit predominates . . . and with some, joy unspeakable and full of glory fills the soul.[74]

There is reflected in this quote an intense yet restrained emotion. His concern for the orderliness of religious worship was a function of his rather staid Presbyterian background, which took literally Paul's injunction that all things in the church were to be done decently and in order. But as Alexander so strongly intimates this does not preclude the presence of fervent emotion which does not trespass the boundaries of propriety in worship. His view on the use and abuse of the principle of sympathy is an illustration of his attempt to do justice to his more formal Presbyterian heritage while acknowledging that the emotions assume a prominent part in one's worship experience.

In light of this discussion Alexander's evaluation of revivalism is seen to be balanced. He was not against revivalism *per se*. What he opposed were those elements in the revivalist movement that made it particularly vulnerable to the charges of appealing merely to man's emotions. Only to speak to the emotions is to treat emotional experience as an end in itself without raising the question whether any specifically Christian element is present as its basis. In the final analysis revivalistic excesses and deviations provide the foil against which true Christian experience is contrasted. It is here that Alexander most consciously attempts to forge a *via media* between a mere doctrinal or confessional approach to Christianity and a strictly emotional or subjective stance.

The guiding maxim of Alexander's positive approach to religious experience was that doctrine and experience are so related as to be complementary. Christian doctrine has specific religious experiences as its counterpart. This is evident from his succinct statements on religious knowledge in his *Thoughts on Religious Experience*. Two kinds of religious knowledge exist "which though intimately connected as cause and effect, may nevertheless be distinguished." The first is the "knowledge of the truth as it is revealed in

---

74. Ibid., pp. 4, 5.

the Holy Scriptures,'' and the second, ''the impression which that truth makes on the human mind when rightly apprehended.''[75] He compares the two to the inscription on a seal and the impression which that seal makes on soft wax. Just as one can inspect the inscription better on the wax than on the seal itself, so the truths of Scripture are confirmed by ''an inward experience of their efficacy on the heart.''[76]

Nevertheless, minds differ so in their ability to apprehend truth and the impressions made on them are often so occluded that ''in judging of religious experience, it is all important to keep steadily in view the system of divine truth, contained in the Holy Scriptures; otherwise, our experience, as is too often the case, will degenerate into enthusiasm.''[77] Spurious experiences must be distinguished from genuine experiences. Nothing was more imperative to Alexander and his successors than to distinguish between true and false experiences and to establish an objective criterion to discern one from the other. This criterion was the Scriptures. ''There is no other test but the infallible word of God; let every thought, motive, impulse and emotion, be brought to this touchstone.''[78] Genuine experience is the result of the Holy Spirit's impressing truths from Scripture on the mind. Knowledge of divine truth is the one thing needful to insure the genuineness of a believer's experience.

> . . . a Knowledge of the truth is essential to genuine piety; error never can, under any circumstances, produce the effects of truth. . . . Any defect in our knowledge of the truth, must, just so far as the error extends, mar the symmetry of the impression produced. . . . There is reason to believe, therefore, that all ignorance of revealed truth, or error respecting it, must be attended with a corresponding defect in the religious exercises of the person.[79]

Alexander's reflection on these themes represents his attempt to formulate a theology of religious experience to reconcile two previously separated traditions. On the one hand he attempts to do justice to his Scotch-Irish Presbyterianism by stressing the importance of doctrinal belief. He spoke approvingly of catechetical instruction of children and of the importance of formal education for ministers. On the other hand Alexander acknowledged the validity of religious experience, specifically conversion experiences

---

75. Ibid., p. 5.
76. Ibid.
77. Ibid., p. 7.
78. Ibid., p. 8; cf. n. 66.
79. Ibid., pp. 8, 9.

which the revivalists stressed. He attempted to combine the best elements from both and to criticize the dangers in accepting the extremes of either position. Alexander's veiled allusion to Presbyterians and their divorce of conversion experience from orthodox theology and his staunch opposition to emotional experiences divorced from a doctrinal basis illustrate the two extremes which were to be avoided at all costs. The confessional element should be prevented from degenerating into mere speculative faith by the insistence that religious conversion is absolutely necessary. The revivalist tradition is safeguarded from enthusiasm by adopting a confessionalism that will provide a distinctly Christian foundation for experience.

Neither tradition is complete without the other, for genuine religious experience has two referents—the objective basis and the experience itself. This distinction was characterized by his oft-repeated differentiation between the head and the heart. The head refers to the cognitive faculty of man which apprehends the truths of Christianity. This objective element is composed of several elements, all or some of which were referred to as the occasion demanded: belief in the historical facts, the scriptural teachings, and various creeds and doctrinal statements in the history of the church. These objective elements are to be believed in the act of saving faith.

The objective act of apprehension and assent is followed by a subjective act of apprehension. A logical as well as a chronological order is manifest. In Alexander's scheme the subjective element could not precede the objective element, for his construction demanded that the objective is the basis for the subjective element. To reverse the order would be to allow the possibility of the experience being founded on the person's natural emotional state. The experience would have no objective anchor either in history, the Scriptures, or doctrine to prevent its being confused with other emotional experiences that are not distinctively Christian. The priority of the objective over the subjective was not due to an inherent inferiority of the subjective, for we have seen that the lack of experience constitutes a serious defect. It is because the subjective element is susceptible to various explanations ranging from differences in temperaments of people and their own natural religious feelings to genuine Christian experiences. On the other hand the objective truths are based on evidence, which were capable of some kind of verification and authentication. Because this was true, the specific facts or truths of Christianity resulted in a specific Christian experience.

This correspondence between the truth and experience received strong emphasis in Alexander's writings and is central to the *via media* that he attempted to forge between his orthodox Presbyterian brethren and the revivalists. In support of his view Alexander cites an extended passage from the leading eighteenth-century advocate of religious experience, Jonathan Edwards. Edwards describes what he experienced when he read I Timothy 1:17: "Now unto the King eternal, immortal, invisible, the only wise God, be honour and glory, for ever and ever, Amen." Alexander quotes Edwards's experience at length:

> As I read these words, there came into my soul, and was as it were diffused through it, a sense of the Divine Being; a new sense; quite different from anything I ever experienced before. Never any words of Scripture seemed to me as those words did. . . . From that time I began to have new kinds of apprehensions and views of Christ, and the work of redemption, and the glorious way of salvation by him. . . . After this my sense of divine things gradually increased, and became more and more lively, and had more of that sweetness.[80]

Edwards's testimony reflects exactly the emphasis of the Princeton professor. The reading and, more importantly, the apprehension of the Scripture was the result of divine illumination, implied by his reference to the newness of the experience. The words of Scripture resulted in new views of Christ. When he apprehended the plan of redemption, his affections were aroused.

Alexander stressed that the specific doctrine or truth apprehended brought a specific response in the affections. Since the objective element is fixed, the experiences of Christians will show remarkable similarities. Foremost among the doctrines in Alexander's illustration of the relation between doctrines and experience are those of sin and Christ. A sense of sin and conviction that one is a sinner is the result of the Holy Spirit's illuminating the law. "If . . . the law is viewed in its spirituality and moral excellence, while there will be experienced an approbation of the will of God thus expressed, yet a lively sense of the sinfulness of our hearts and lives must be the predominant feeling."[81] Therefore, all acts of faith that involve the law of God will be accompanied with "painful emotions, on account of the deep conviction of disconformity to that perfect rule, which cannot but be experienced, when that object is before the mind."[82] The affective response of

---

80. Ibid., p.42. Although Alexander does not mention the source, this quotation is from Edwards's *Personal Narrative*. It is interesting that Alexander takes this quotation in which Edwards discusses his perception of the glory of God in *nature* and uses it for his own purposes—i.e., to illustrate spiritual apprehension of *doctrine*.

81. Ibid., p. 95.

82. Ibid., p. 96.

the feelings is determined by the truth which is apprehended by the mind. On the more positive side, views of Christ result in experiences of joy.

But all those invitations, promises, and declarations which exhibit a Saviour, and the method of recovery, when truly believed . . . must be accompanied, not only with love, but joy, and hope, and a free consent to be saved in God's appointed way; and when the previous distress and discouragement have been great, and the views of the gospel clear, the joy is overflowing, and as long as these views are unclouded, peace flows like a river.[83]

Alexander's references to Christ and His work were always couched in language that suggests a fervent piety. Sometimes the language even suggests an immediacy bordering on the mystical.

Alexander's description of how apprehension of truth gives rise to religious experience falls somewhere between what might crudely be described as "stimulus and response" and a contemplative experience. The former imagery is not altogether inappropriate since Alexander asserts that apprehension is the occasion which almost triggers an emotional response. That his view does not really fit such a crude description is evident from other passages where an element of contemplation and meditation are involved. Meditation is not simply a matter of stimulus (reading a particular scriptural passage) and response (feeling the appropriate religious affection), but an experience that can only be attributed to the Holy Spirit's illuminating the mind. The very fact that the work of the Spirit results in new views supports the possibility that the Spirit is involved in the religious experience. This contemplative aspect also prohibits our interpreting an almost mechanical working between doctrine and feelings.

That the apprehension of truth and its accompanying experience is the essence of piety does not imply that every individual is bound to have the same experience to the same degree of emotional intensity in comparison with either another *individual's* apprehension or one's own apprehension of the same truth at another *time*. Great variety characterizes different experiences due to the clarity of apprehension and the truth viewed. While a general similarity in experience is present, diversity is thus allowed.[84] The general similarity of experience, however, is a witness against enthusiasm

---

83. Ibid.
84. That Alexander allows for diversity of experience is evident from the many narratives of various individuals' experiences, which he adduces and analyzes. Whole chapters in *Thoughts* are devoted to individual experiences.

which Alexander contends "assumes a thousand different shapes and hues, and is marked by no uniform characteristics."[85] Thus scriptural piety is the same whether one examines the old dispensation (David), the New Testament (Paul), or figures from the rest of church history—the Fathers, the Reformers, and the Puritans. Such diversity as exists is due to a lack of clearness in the apprehension of the truth or a failure to see all the truths in their natural relations.

Defects in piety are produced by defects in apprehension. This led Alexander to express perhaps the only criticisms in all his writings against the Reformers and the Puritans. Because their vision was limited to doing battle with Rome, the Reformers neglected other areas. Their piety was "pure and vigorous, but not as expansive as it might have been. They seem scarcely to have thought of the hundreds of millions of heathen in the world; and of course made no efforts to extend the knowledge of salvation to them."[86] Even controversies among the Reformers diffused a zeal that could have been more profitably directed in reaching the lost. The Puritans also lacked this expansiveness but God's providence overruled so that when they were forbidden to preach they took to writing works that have been used evangelistically. Whatever we think about Alexander's oversimplification of the history of piety and his view of the rest of history from the pinnacle of the nineteenth century, his attempt to see common elements in various periods of history is indicative of his conciliatory attitude.

Considering all of Alexander's theology, his views of revivals are correlative to his views of religious experience. Alexander outlined the prerequisites for genuine revival. Of first importance is that the gospel be preached in its purity. The ideal situation is one in which the community has been previously well instructed in the doctrines of Christianity. Those who have been well catechized will have experiences which are much purer than those who are generally ignorant of the truths of the Bible. True revival takes place when people are well prepared: "The word of God distils upon the mind like gentle rain, and the Holy Spirit comes down like a dew, diffusing a blessed influence all around. Its aspect gives us a lively idea of what will be the general state of things IN THE LATTER DAY GLORY. . . ."[87]

In genuine revivals intense feeling and emotion are present with a singular lack in wild outbursts. The feelings are just as fervent as in meetings where

---

85. "Nature of Vital Piety," p. 13.
86. Ibid., p. 22.
87. "Letter," p. 4.

emotion is unrestrained, but the atmosphere, conducive to genuine work of the Spirit, provides less opportunity for mere sympathetic mimicry to occur. A spirit of devotion is enkindled. The word of God becomes exceedingly precious. Prayer is the exercise in which the soul seems to be in its proper element . . . God is approached, and his presence felt, and beauty seen; and the new-born soul lives by breathing after the knowledge of God, after communion with God, and after conformity to his will.[88]

This led Alexander to ponder the possibility of a state of the church in which seasons of revival were not necessary. He was not advocating a Bushnellian rejection of conversion. Rather he wanted to eliminate the evils that always attended "temporary excitements," specifically the "deplorable state of declension, and disgraceful apathy and inactivity" which followed sporadic outbursts almost as regularly as winter follows summer. The ideal state would be that of continuous genuine revival in which sinners were constantly being converted. "Why may we not hope for such a state of increasing prosperity in the church, that *revivals* shall not be needed or if you prefer the expression, when there shall be a *perpetual revival.*"[89] He alludes to reports that for a sustained period of time such was the case for two Puritan pastors. Nevertheless, he acknowledges that such a desire would be setting man's will up above God's will since it seems to be God's good pleasure to send seasons of refreshing. If the Sovereign "chooses to water his church by occasional showers, rather than the perpetual dew of his grace . . . we should rejoice and be grateful for the rich effusions of his Spirit in any form and manner. . . ."[90] The obligation of Christians is to benefit from such periods and use them for the conversion of sinners and the edification of the saints.

Summary of Alexander's Formal Writings on Religious Experience

Alexander's two-front attack in the area of religious experience established a pattern that was to be the permanent Princeton model for any discussion of religious experience. His purpose was to forge a *via media* between a cold speculation and a burning enthusiasm. However, Alexander

88. Ibid., p. 5.
89. Ibid.
90. Ibid., p. 6. Charles Hodge noted that Alexander stressed in one of his sermons that it was an "awful error to oppose revivals," thus confirming that what Alexander advocated was continuous revival without attendant emotional excesses and subsequent declension ("Dr. Alexander's Sermons," p. 40).

clearly established the priorities by declaring the objective element as the foundation for the subjective. The reasons for this priority stem from their adherence to the Scripture as God's authoritative Word to man. Nevertheless, Alexander also showed a preoccupation with the question of religious experience and staunchly contended that Presbyterian orthodoxy must be united with a vital piety. Subjective experience must be present for genuine Christianity to exist even if experience was to be subordinate to the test of Scripture. Without devotion Christianity is reduced to the level of the speculative philosophies. Alexander's own fervent piety was evident not only when discussing experience directly and advocating conversion as a *sine qua non* of Christianity but appeared even in the midst of his writings that show scholastic overtones. His writings on the revivals were temperate, but he was adamantly opposed to their excesses. He was equally opposed to certain of his orthodox brethren whose emphasis on doctrine often left no room for experience, but his criticisms of them were more veiled.

Alexander contended that one's views on religious experience were to be gathered partly from experience and partly from the Scriptures. The former was emphasized in this study to illustrate Alexander's heavy dependence on experience. Alexander's dependence on the Scriptures is well established as well as the fact that his views were partially shaped from controversy. The motive lying behind this study is not to establish Alexander's emphasis on the objective elements in religious experience, which are obvious, but to highlight his intense interest in the subjective element and the integration of the latter with the former. Alexander's strong predilection with the concerns of experience are even more strikingly evident in his devotional writings to which we shall now turn.

Alexander's Devotional Writings

According to Alexander's friends and colleagues his devotional writings, particularly his sermons, were the most influential of all his writings. Charles Hodge's open admiration for his close friend was no more apparent than when he spoke of Alexander's ability in preaching to call forth the religious emotions. His particular gift in Hodge's opinion was to search a man's heart and to aid him in introspection. "As with a lighted torch he would lead a man through the labyrinth of his heart, in places which his intelligent consciousness had never entered."[91] Three sermons were par-

---

91. "A Discourse Delivered at the Re-opening of the Chapel," p. 22. According to Hodge's son it was reported that Alexander's knowledge and description of the unconverted heart led a

ticularly memorable to Hodge. In them Alexander's power of description was such that the hearers felt as if they were present at the scenes described. "We left the Chapel after his sermon on the transfiguration, feeling that we had seen the Lord in his glory, at least as through a glass darkly." A sermon on Christ's passion made such an impact that students wondered about the mystery of its power. Hodge said of it "I do not think that it was printed; but the manuscript came into our hands; and when I read it, there was nothing there, but what is in the Gospels. So that the mystery of its power remained unsolved."[92] Such praise bordering on ascribing inspiration was characteristic of the Princeton men despite their strong opposition to Quakerism. A. A. Hodge commenting on Alexander's Sunday conferences said:

> Drawing the large Bible down before him, he seemed to lose at once all sense of human audience, and to pass alone into the presence of God. . . . A solemn hush fell over us, and we felt not as those who listen to a teacher, but as those who are admitted to approach, with the shoes from off their feet, to gaze in and listen through an open window to the mysterious workings of a sanctified soul under the immediate revelations of the Holy Ghost.[93]

That is strong language for a Princeton divine!

Alexander's son describes his father's role as a preacher and his effectiveness as an orator. From the time of his missionary journeys as a young man his forte was preaching. Despite his youthful age of twenty his preaching was effective and well received.[94] According to his son, Alexander excelled in two kinds of discourse: doctrinal and experiential.

> . . . he set forth the whole system of Divine truth, with a felicitous mixture of doctrine and experience; not separately but intimately blended; the didactic ways being traversed by a woof of variegated emotion; the steel links of reasoning being often red with ardours of burning love.[95]

In the *Life of Archibald Alexander* numerous references testify to Alexander's gift of appealing to the emotions of his hearers. While his purpose never was to arouse emotional outbursts, occasionally a "half suppressed

---

noted figure from the town of Princeton to surmise that "Dr. Alexander must have been very wicked in his youth, or he could not know so well how wicked men felt" (*Life of Charles Hodge*, p. 27).
92. Ibid.
93. *LCH*, pp. 456, 457.
94. *LAA*, p. 142.
95. Ibid., p. 687. Cf. pp. 172, 423, 424, 686.

sob'' was heard.[96] Thus in his preaching the Princeton pastor attempted to live up to the ideal, which we noted above, that where genuine religious worship takes place a true sympathy is aroused among the hearers such that affections are stimulated but still restrained, befitting the occasion of divine worship.

The occasions for Alexander's preaching were not only appointed intervals in the seminary and college chapel but invitations from community churches as well. He preached most movingly as far as students were concerned in the Sunday afternoon conferences in the oratory. While the classroom was devoted to the cultivation of intellectual pursuits, the conferences were "directed solely to the cultivation of the heart. . . ."[97] The conferences were organized to suit Alexander's abilities in extemporaneous, experiential preaching. Singing and prayer preceded a discussion of a subject in practical religion. Students began the discussion with the professors following in ascending order of rank. These discussions on vital piety shaped the spiritual tone of the seminary.

It is with some hesitation that we turn to examine Alexander's sermons. His son asserts that he either slavishly followed the manuscript, in which case the reader fails to get a true impression of his extemporaneous preaching, or, as was more often the case, he used it only sparingly in the form of a scrap of notes taken into the pulpit. The written sermons, according to his son lacked "the illustrations, descriptions, flight and pathos of his free productions."[98] Nevertheless, since some of the manuscripts are fully 35 handwritten pages and more, indicating the efforts expended on their writing, and since he often resorted to manuscripts on many occasions, and finally since his sermons bear out his more systematic writings, we will examine them.

The most striking characteristic of the more than 100 manuscripts is the profusion of Scripture passages written verbatim. In a sermon on Psalm 97:1 one section containing 132 lines has 97 that are verbatim quotes from other Bible passages virtually strung together like an anthology of verses on a subject.[99] Since the Scripture is the means by which we come to know Christ, Alexander coupled the Scriptures with his preaching to use the only means by which genuine religious faith is communicated. The Scriptures are

96. Ibid., p. 411.
97. Ibid., p. 420.
98. Ibid., p. 688.
99. "Sermons," "Psa. 97:1, 'The Lord Reigneth, let the earth rejoice'" (n.p.).

of the utmost importance because they provide a safeguard against substituting mere figments of the imagination.

Defect in Christian experience is prevented by holding carefully to sound doctrine, specifically what Alexander called "fundamental doctrines." Two characteristics distinguish fundamental doctrines: 1. "That the denial of them destroys the system. 2. That the knowledge of them is essential to piety."[100] In this description Alexander succinctly captures the essence of the Princeton theology and the Princeton piety. In juxtaposing doctrine and piety in this way Alexander continues the Reformed tradition extending back to John Calvin himself. Recent studies have stressed the relation between piety and doctrine as the foundation of Calvin's *Institutes* and his abhorrence of speculative method when dealing with the study of God.[101]

In his sermons Alexander reiterated his view of religious experience espoused in his systematic writings. While he affirmed the legitimate role of emotions, he opposed outbursts of the affections. In a sermon on III John 2 he even asserted that the true character of a man is dependent on his affections' direction and strength: ". . . if men would know what is the state of their spiritual health let them examine into the state of their affections. . . ."[102] Two extremes indicate danger. A complete lack of feeling is the danger at one extreme. On the other hand if believer's affections are "irregular, feverish, and misdirected" he errs to the opposite extreme. By encouraging emotional outbursts, many claim to manifest true love of God while in reality they demonstrate only "the mere stirrings of natural passions. The flight of a heated imagination and even feelings which belong entirely to our animal nature have been dignified with this name."[103] However, certain characteristics always seem to pertain to those who exhibit great emotions. A lack of permanence is in direct proportion to their violence. The more zealous and inflamed the emotions, the more likely the experience is to decline. Though genuine experience often appears inferior in comparison with enthusiasm, the latter is like the meteors which outshine the stars for a while, only to fade away. The zeal of true Christian experience

100. Ibid., "II Timothy 2:15 'Study to shew Thyself. . . .' " (n.p.).
101. Cf. John T. McNeill's Introduction, section VIII, to the Battles translation, *Calvin: Institutes of the Christian Religion*, Westminster, 1960 and Ford Lewis Battles and Stanley Tagg, *The Piety of John Calvin*, 1978.
102. "Sermons," "III John 2."
103. Ibid., "John 27:17, 'Simon . . . lovest thou me?' " Cf. *Practical Sermons*, pp. 262, 502.

is permanent and is exhibited in a continual devotional spirit.[104]

The sermon best illustrating Alexander's preaching on experience is on Colossians 1:27, "Christ in you the hope of glory." The biblical passage admits of a certain mystical element, and the meaning of "being in Christ" or "abiding in him" is only fully apprehended in the experience of it. The union of the believer and Christ is "intimate, spiritual, mystical, and indissoluble."[105] This union results in communion with Christ "such as that which is experienced in the living human body, between the head and the members, which are so united, as to be animated with one common principle of life."[106] Union with Christ does not result from orthodox opinions alone, which can be likened to a speculative knowledge. This knowledge is "correct as far as it goes," but it fails to reach that knowledge resulting from seeing "the King in his beauty."[107] Those who have experienced this vision sense the barrenness of mere speculation. The true believer embraces Christ "by the full consent of the will, and supreme attachment of the affections." Alexander even goes to the extent of saying that "it is peculiarly and eminently in the affections that Christ dwells. Here is his throne in the human heart. Here he reigns as King, and he must have no rival."[108]

Alexander explicates this by saying that this union is manifest by the love of Christ in the heart and life of the believer. Many confuse this with their own emotions or a general respect for religion. However, if Christ is really in the believer, "we shall love him for his own sake." The object of this love is "the excellence of his character, the beauty of his holiness."[109] That this love has more personal characteristics is indicated by his calling the relationship one of communion.

> If Christ be in us there will be communion. . . . He will sometimes speak to us—He will speak comfortably to us—He will give tokens of his love. He will invite our confidence and will shed abroad his love in our hearts. And if Christ be formed within us we cannot remain altogether ignorant of his presence. Our hearts, while he communes with us, will sometimes ["often" is crossed out!] burn within us.[110]

---

104. Ibid., "John 27:17, 'Simon . . . lovest thou me?' " Cf. also "Charge Delivered to J. Jones at his Ordination."
105. Ibid., "Col. 1:27, 'Christ in you the hope of glory,' " p. 2. Cf. *Practical Sermons*, p. 201.
106. Ibid.
107. Ibid., p. 10. Cf. p. 142.
108. Ibid., pp. 11, 12.
109. Ibid., p. 12.
110. Ibid., pp. 13, 14.

However, Alexander then shifts to a more contemplative experience. He exhorts the believer to contemplate Christ's divine characteristics, which leads to an experience of appreciation and confidence in his work. But Alexander broaches the personal element again as well: "We shall rejoice to lean upon his arm—to pour the sorrows of our hearts into his bosom—The soul in which he dwells . . . will feel itself to be entirely his. . . ."[111]

With the introduction of personal communion new light is shed on Alexander's view as to just how religious experience arises from doctrine. From the sermon just examined two elements are closely related—the contemplative and the communal. The contemplative strand is related to the knowledge of doctrine which in turn provides the basis for any genuine religious experience. Contemplation sets the stage for the element of communion or we might say the cognitive element precedes the affective. The believer accepts the Scriptures as a guide to contemplate all the aspects of the Christian faith. This ranges from doctrinal statements about the decrees of God and the plan of salvation to the being of God Himself and the person and work of Christ. For example, the mere contemplation of the law and the work of Christ was to produce an effect in the emotions. Such contemplation surpasses mere intellectual or speculative knowledge. But the additional element of communion brings a still deeper dimension to the experience. The sermon passages adduced above suggest an immediacy of personal communion between the believer and Christ. It is the ultimate goal toward which the element of trust and confidence in saving faith point. The believer begins to know God and Christ in a way that mere speculative knowledge can never begin to comprehend. Alexander cannot describe this in detail for the whole concept of union with Christ can be known only by experience. When he makes descriptive statements about this relationship, he falls back into the contemplative strand. This is not to say that it is inferior, for Alexander does not make the distinction between contemplative knowledge and knowledge by communion which we have made for purposes of analysis. No indications are present that Alexander was ever aware that these two themes are distinguishable in his thought. Knowledge by contemplation is obviously the dominant motif in his writings. It is only occasionally that this other element appears and even then it is not without an admixture of contemplative elements.

Justifications for Alexander's emphasis on the contemplative strand are obvious from the rest of his writings on experience. Since the Scriptures and

---

111. Ibid., p. 14.

other statements of faith provide the starting point for the contemplative experience, knowledge by contemplation precedes and determines the character of any experience of communion with Christ. Despite this regulative principle, the possibility of personal communion with Christ opens an experiential area which he never fully develops. Alexander accounts for this by saying that union with Christ is fully known only by experience. That the experience is always subject to the test of the Scriptures does not fully suppress the strength of the subjective element in Alexander's thought. We find still other passages that seem to be within the borders of mystical experiences.

Such passages are rare in Alexander's writings; yet mystical phrases and vocabulary are to be found. In "Love to an Unseen Savior," a tract for the Presbyterian Board of Education, Alexander discusses the subject of religious feeling and particularly the theme of the Christian's ardent desire to be in the presence of God that he might become more conformed to the image of Christ. All of the traits of Christ appear pleasing to the believer: "One bright view of his excellence and beauty ravishes the soul with unspeakable delight." Indeed if we love Him unseen, "how strong will be our love when we shall see him face to face, and find ourselves not only in his real presence, but enclosed in his affectionate embrace."[112] While it is true that Alexander places this experience in the context of the future, heavenly state, yet the language used is peculiar for him.

In a sermon on Luke 10:42 entitled "One thing is needful . . ." Alexander discusses the nearness of Christians to Christ.

> They delight in retirement because there in secret silence of the mind, there is often an opportunity of conversing with their Savior. If we could penetrate the clouds of their pious souls, we should often find them in company with Mary at the feet of Jesus, as it were, washing them with their penitential and grateful tears.[113]

While this passage may not be as suggestive as the former ones, the idea of intimate communion with Christ to the point of conversation with Him is strongly presented.

The most forceful of all the mystical overtones is found, strangely

---

112. "Love to an Unseen Savior," pp. 7, 8. The term "mystical" is used advisedly since Alexander would have strongly opposed the concept of the absorption of the individual into God, which is characteristic of much mystical thought. Nevertheless, the erotic vocabulary that Alexander employs is such that "mystical" is not wholly misleading.

113. "Sermons," "Luke 10:42, 'One thing is needful . . .' " (n.p.).

enough, in an article in the *Princeton Review,* "Evidences of a New Heart."
The article is mainly a straightforward discussion of evidences, quite usual
for Alexander. The evidences are a sincere love toward God with accompanying affections in the heart. Another evidence is the desire for
communion with God and enjoyment of God's presence. He seems to be
sensitive to the tender consciences of many Christians and thus tempers this
last statement.

> We might discourage and distress the timid Christian, by laying down
> the sensible enjoyment of communion with God as an inseparable
> attendant on piety . . . but certainly we must insist on *the desire, the
> habitual* desire of such communion, as an evidence of piety. . . .[114]

But in discussing the enjoyment of God's presence Alexander expresses
deep feeling:

> We need say nothing about the joy experienced from the sensible
> manifestation of God's presence, and from the light of his countenance
> lifted up on the soul; for these our aid is not needed, for the soul enjoys
> already a blessed assurance of the divine favour, and is not only
> conscious of loving God, but feels the *love of God* shed abroad in the
> heart, and can say in the language of the spouse, *my beloved is mine and
> I am his.*[115]

From the casual way in which he introduces this experience it would appear
that Alexander expected this to be the normal experience of Christians.
These passages are never developed any more fully in the rest of his
writings. However, they indicate the scope of Alexander's own experience
of intense piety. Since the knowledge that Alexander advocates in the bulk
of his writings suggests a kind of propositional approach to revelation, we
might be surprised that such a mystical element is to be found. However, it is
not incongruent once we understand that in Alexander's thought contemplative knowledge naturally runs into knowledge by communion. What might
be interpreted by some as strictures in the objective element, i.e., assent not
only to promises but also to historical and doctrinal facts, did not at all
appear limiting to Alexander, whose own piety apparently included experiences akin to the mystical. Contemplative knowledge gives rise to knowledge by communion. The presence of a distinction in Alexander's view of
experience between what can be expressed in words and the mystery of

114. "Evidences of a New Heart," *Biblical Repertory and Theological Review,* VI, 1834,
p. 357.
115. Ibid.

communion with God is analogous to Calvin's expression of his inadequacy to articulate the mystery of communion with God through the Lord's Supper. Speaking of the mystery of union with Christ, Calvin doubts that it can be reduced to words.

> I therefore freely admit that no man should measure its sublimity by the little measure of my childishness. Rather, I urge my readers not to confine their mental interest within these too narrow limits, but to strive to rise much higher than I can lead them. . . . Although my mind can think beyond what my tongue can utter, yet even my mind is conquered and overwhelmed by the greatness of the thing.[116]

Two examples can be cited from Alexander's writings which underscore the profound regard that he accorded to the feelings or emotions despite his subordination of them to the objective elements of the Christian faith. They are singular because they run counter to the usual scheme the Princeton pastor outlines; i.e., knowledge of the objective element illuminated by the Holy Spirit precedes the subjective element. In "Communion—The Difference between Christian and Church Fellowship" Alexander used a phrase that the Princeton school usually avoided: "Theology of the intellect and theology of the feelings." The article discusses Baptists who advocated close communion. They refused either to admit believers who had never been baptized by immersion or to take communion in congregations where immersion was not practiced. Many believers chafed under such restrictions. They enjoyed fellowship with believers in other denominations and yet had to abstain from taking part in their communion because of their doctrinal stance. A believer might realize in his heart that "his heart is with them but his adopted creed says 'Touch not—handle not'; you must not commune in the Lord's Supper with these lambs of Christ."[117] That some would disobey their theology of the intellect and follow the theology of the heart should not be surprising.

> [The exclusive principle] violates the best and warmest feelings of piety; and often when from argument or it is believed to be necessary, it is difficult to keep a heart with brotherly affection from rising in revulsion against the exclusive principle.[118]

Alexander cited the case of a Rev. John Weatherford who was called to account for communing with Presbyterians.

---

116. *Institutes of the Christian Religion*, IV, 17, 7.
117. "Communion . . ." *Princeton Review*, 22, no. 4 (1850): 559.
118. Ibid., p. 560.

On being arraigned, he candidly confessed that, overcome by his feelings, he had acted contrary to his cool judgment of what was proper, and expressed sorrow for the offence to his brethren. Oh what a humiliation. He never could repent of the feelings which impelled him, nor of the act of obeying the command of his Saviour.[119]

It is clear that in this situation the intellectual element was defective. Therefore, the subjective feelings took the lead and became the determining factor thus correcting an error in the theology of the intellect. This is in direct opposition to the usual scheme of Christian experience. Alexander considered this a correct usage of the distinction between a theology of the intellect and a theology of the feeling. When situations arise in which the intellectual element, which Alexander associates with the objective element in experience, is faulty, then the religious feelings may provide the necessary corrective. This represents a flexibility in his theology.

The other noteworthy example of an inverted order of objective and subjective elements is Alexander's introductory remarks to a collection of hymns he compiled. In the introduction he explains the value of hymns to pious Christians and rehearses the various uses that can be made of them in an individual's religious life. The collection of hymns in his opinion is suitable for "all persons of evangelical views and pious feelings." This fact is supported by the further observation that even those "who seem to be wide apart in regard to many speculative points, can often harmonize in their devotional exercises."[120] Alexander's latitude at this juncture indicates a tolerant attitude toward those who did not agree with him in the very important area of Christian doctrine.

. . . Christians frequently differ more from each other in appearance than in reality: for they who can sincerely and cordially unite in the same prayers, and in the same spiritual songs, must be of one heart and one mind in all that constitutes the essence of religion.[121]

God has ordained the use of music as a vehicle of the gospel, especially to the young and ignorant. He contends that the uneducated retain more of the gospel through the proliferation of gospel songs than by any other means, including preaching. But the truly startling principle is that "the understanding is reached with most certainty through the feelings of the heart. The mind

119. Ibid., p. 561.
120. *A Selection of Hymns, Adapted to the Devotions of the Closet, the Family, and the Social Circle* . . . , p. iv.
121. Ibid.

must be excited and warmed before it will receive the distinct and indelible impressions of the truth.''[122] This is no more profoundly illustrated, he states, than by the revivalists' use of songs to perform the strategic function of preparing the hearts of the hearers to receive the gospel message: ''. . . the sentiments and feelings of young converts is as much moulded by these songs of Zion, which at such seasons are so frequently sung, as by all the discourses which are heard from the pulpit.''[123]

The application of this principle of emotional preparation for the reception of truth is not limited to public worship. It can be used by the believer in his devotional life as well. "Indeed, there is no situation in which the heart is likely to be more susceptible to the softening and elevating effects of sacred music, than in the solemn stillness of solitude."[124] Some people have indicated in their diaries that they have literally sung their private devotions to themselves using no prepared tune but simply following their feelings. They have found this "an excellent method of fixing the attention and exciting the devout emotions of the heart."[125] Without some means such as music, believers often have difficulty in safeguarding their minds from wandering thoughts and even hardness or dullness of heart. Believers should avail themselves of all legitimate means to stir up their hearts in times of spiritual declension. Because there is a judicious blend of gospel truth and piety written in a pleasing style, "a fine effect is produced on the pious heart, by the mere perusal of them."[126] Alexander concludes that because sacred songs can fulfill this important task, tract societies should note this "taste for poetry" and avail themselves of this means of spreading the gospel.

It is clear that Alexander has departed in these instances from his original scheme. According to the majority of his teaching the objective serves as the foundation for the subjective in religious experience. The reading and understanding of the Scriptures or doctrine precedes the experiential element. If doctrine does not precede emotional experience, the believer is susceptible to the danger of having an experience devoid of distinctively Christian characteristics. However, in these instances the order has been explicitly reversed. Owing to man's dullness of heart and want of devotional motivation Alexander contends that man's heart has to be softened before he is taught doctrine to believe. His original thesis is not radically altered,

---

122. Ibid., p. vii.
123. Ibid.
124. Ibid , p. x.
125. Ibid. Cf. *Practical Sermons*, p. 305.
126. Ibid., p. xii.

however, since it is from reading hymns embodying the truths of the gospel that the emotions are stimulated. It is not merely music that puts him "in the mood," as it were, for the reception of doctrine. Rather it is almost an aesthetic intuition instigated by the apprehension of biblical truth in poetic form. This reveals how intertwined in Alexander's thought are the objective and subjective elements in Christian experience. On occasions the subjective precedes the objective chronologically, but the order is usually reversed. Nevertheless, it is inconceivable to him that one will be isolated from the other. To have one to the exclusion of the other is to ignore the wholeness of man in his religious experience. The head without the heart is cold and devoid of life; the heart without the head is mere animal emotionalism.

One final illustration of Alexander's practical emphasis of experience is the way he deftly employed the principle of sympathy in his preaching style. At first glance the majority of his sermons are merely expositions of the text. The main interest was elaboration of Scripture for its doctrinal significance. Only rarely, however, does he delve into technical problems. At the end of his sermons he included a section entitled "implications," "reflections," or "inferences" which summarized and drew practical implications from the passage. Usually the section contained practical exhortations implied in the biblical text.

Occasionally this hortatory part of the sermon included strongly emotional appeals, particularly when Alexander dealt with a passage on death, judgment, or impenitence. Frequently the appeal appeared as a long series of questions encouraging the sinner to examine his soul's condition.

Are any of us, in this assembly, in the "gall of bitterness and bond of iniquity?" . . . Are any of you in an unconverted state? . . . And if you should die tonight, does conscience tell you that you are unprepared for heaven? Think then of your sad condition. There may be but a step between you and death. . . . Seize the present moment. . . . Tomorrow it may be too late.[127]

Alexander often preached on death and deathbed experiences. Fully seven out of 22 chapters in *Thoughts on Religious Experience* are devoted to this subject. He included a lengthy prayer for those approaching death to use as a guide. He believed that deathbed experiences of believers are the most convincing of all arguments for Christianity. In the sermons he preached at funerals Alexander usually mentioned how the deceased approached death.

127. *Practical Sermons*, pp. 494-95. Cf. p. 125; also *Practical Truths*, pp. 96-100.

He often repeated glowing words of testimony which he witnessed.

These sermons and his use of sympathy in preaching are another indication of the strong emotional appeal Alexander made in his sermons. He would deny that such an emphasis violated any fundamental principle in the rest of his thoughts regarding the role of emotions in religion, and it is obvious that such methods were in keeping with his own inward piety. Yet when such weight is attached to this particular practice there is a certain logical inconsistency with the scheme that he insisted was the correct one, i.e., that the objective element precedes logically and chronologically the subjective element. That such preaching methods and passages containing an inverted sequence would not seem incongruous to the Princeton professor was due to his seeing doctrinal and experience all of one piece. Emotional exhortations were never preached without having first preached the biblical message of life after death through Christ. Even when hymns were suggested to soften the hearts of the hearers, they were thoroughly evangelical in their content. Orthodoxy and experience were always bedfellows to Alexander and his goal as the "pastor" at Princeton was to assure that the marriage was a long and successful one.

In forging a *via media* between orthodox Presbyterian confessionalism and revivalist enthusiasm Alexander attempted to draw on the best and put aside the worst aspects of each position. He was not always successful at the latter as traces of scholastic methodology and rationalistic presuppositions often assume a place of prominence in his thinking. Whether this was to give the impression that serious intellectual work was being accomplished at Princeton in training men who were converted in the revivals is impossible to say. What is clear is that Alexander was not paying lip service to the revivalist faction in the Presbyterian church in order to keep the fold together. His own religious experience was too influential for him to disparage revivalism altogether. While some of his writings and practices show traces of inconsistency, these are overshadowed, even obliterated, by his attempt to unite the best elements from the two camps of Presbyterianism. Conversion experience is not only valid; it is an indispensable element arising out of the content of the gospel.

In describing his position Alexander drew from his own experience and the Bible. His sermons were eminently logical discourses enlivened by appeals and exhortations calculated to arouse a response from his hearers. If on occasion mystical elements appeared, the doctrinal moorings were not far off. The Princeton piety was to be established so that its graduates were to be "eminently logical divines" who at the same time were men of "pious affections and tender feelings." Not only were the theological and philosophical foundations well established by Alexander but the experimental as well. The stage was well prepared for Alexander's prize pupil and *the* theologian of the Princeton school, Charles Hodge.

CHAPTER TWO

CHARLES HODGE: PRINCETON THEOLOGIAN

Charles Hodge is the central figure in any discussion of the Princeton theology. Through the publications of his voluminous *Systematic Theology*, his editorship of the *Princeton Review* from its inception in 1825 until 1871 when he retired as editor, his preaching of hundreds of sermons both in the Princeton community and neighboring churches, and his personal piety, his influence was to spread literally around the world. Approximately 3000 students sat under his tutelage at Princeton, the majority of whom became ministers in the Presbyterian church.

Historians and theologians have usually stressed his defense and propagation of Calvinism, and the strong intellectual bent in his teaching as his primary emphasis. However, a perusal of the memorial addresses written by those closest to him and the reviews of his career as a teacher reveals an aspect of his character and influence which appears to be antithetical to the intellectualism stressed by many critics. Robert Hastings Nichols in his article on Hodge in the *Dictionary of American Biography* affirms the presence of intellectualism in Hodge's work. Hodge's teaching exhibited "solid learning, acquaintance with continental thought . . . strong certainty, clear analytical statements, and skill in awakening minds."[1] However in terms of total impact upon those whom he taught, Hodge's personal piety was of still greater import.

> Even more influential, however, was his personal religion, evinced especially in his famous Sunday afternoon conference addresses. His real and strongly emotional piety, the heart of which was vital apprehension of the love of God in Christ, wrought his most characteristic work upon his students.[2]

Sometimes the contrast between Hodge's theology and method and his personal qualities were juxtaposed in a striking way: "In him it was conspicuously seen, how warm and loving a heart may beat beneath what some

---

1. 9: 68.
2. Ibid.

would regard as the cold steel of a Calvinistic coat of mail.''[3]
If Alexander was the "pastor" of the Princeton school, Hodge was its theologian. He alone of the three men produced a *Systematic Theology*. While all three men were professors of theology, Hodge was the one who immortalized the school's thought in volumes that are still reprinted in the latter part of the twentieth century. David Wells has therefore characterized Hodge's theology as "stout and persistent."[4] Wells contends that Hodge's theology and his reputation as a theologian have endured because of the remarkable mixture of piety and learning that is diffused in his work.

We find his work an almost classic realization of the kneeling, as opposed to sitting theologian. He had seen the grace and glory of God, and in his *Systematic Theology* he turns to the world to explain his vision.[5]

Our purpose in this chapter is to present Charles Hodge as exemplified by these remarks. In order to do this we will examine passages from his biography and his letters and journals as well as his systematic works to ascertain the nature of his own religious experience. We will find that his piety was of such a nature as to influence profoundly his theology, both in its method and content.

Hodge's Personal Religious Experience

The personal religious experience of Charles Hodge differs considerably from Archibald Alexander's. Such differences stem from a dissimilarity not only in family background but in his whole training. Both had definite effects on Hodge's approach to religious experience. He was born in 1797, the fifth of five children in a very strong Presbyterian family in Philadelphia. Hodge's piety was shaped during his childhood days by his mother, who raised the children alone since her husband died a year after Charles was born. Charles's admiration for his mother was profound: "To our mother, my brother and myself, under God, owe absolutely everything. To us she devoted her life. For us she prayed, labored, and suffered."[6] Mary Hodge took the children to church regularly and "drilled" them in the Westminster

3. C. A. Salmond, *Princetonia: Charles and A. A. Hodge; with Class and Table Talk of Hodge the Younger*, p. 33.
4. "The Stout and Persistent 'Theology' of Charles Hodge," *Christianity Today* (Aug. 30, 1974), p. 10.
5. Ibid., p. 12.
6. *Life of Charles Hodge*, p.9, hereafter *LCH*.

Catechism. In an autobiographical sketch included in *The Life of Charles Hodge* written by his son, Hodge described his religious experiences as a child:

> There has never been anything remarkable in my religious experience, unless it be that it began very early. I think that in my childhood I came nearer to conforming to the apostle's injunction: "Pray without ceasing," than in any other period of my life. As far back as I can remember, I had the habit of thanking God for everything I received, and asking him for everything I wanted. If I lost a book, or any of my playthings, I prayed that I might find it. I prayed walking along the streets, in school and out of school, whether playing or studying. I did not do this in obedience to any prescribed rule. It seemed natural. I thought of God as an everywhere-present Being, full of kindness and love, who would not be offended if children talked to him.[7]

He compared these prayers to the worship which the birds offered to God. To such a faith Hodge attributed his having used profanity but once in his life. Hodge refers to these childhood experiences as a "mild form of natural religion,"[8] yet they reveal the beginnings of a personal religious life which was only to be deepened as the years passed.

While attending Princeton Hodge had a conversion experience, in 1815. It was not accompanied by a very dramatic change in his life since the conversion had as its foundation not only the memorized Westminster Catechism but a religious disposition against which he never seemed to have rebelled at all. Even though Hodge tended to play down the revivalistic excitement which swept the campus (in letters he said the reports of revival at Princeton tended to be exaggerated), he did not oppose such conversion experiences and the revival itself.

During the latter part of his seminary preparation he was engaged in missionary work by preaching on Sundays. At this time he kept the only religious diary he ever wrote. Several entries indicate the intensity of his concern regarding his own religious experience or lack thereof.

> On Wednesday evening, October 20th, 1819, I preached my trial sermon at Pittsgrove. . . . Though the Lord had kindly afforded me solemn feelings in view of my entrance on the ministry, yet I found my heart but little engaged during the time of the service.
>
> Nov. 28th, 1819. . . . During this sacred day I have experienced very little spiritual enjoyment; my heart has been too far from God. . . .Let

---

7. Ibid., p. 13.
8. Ibid.

not, my soul, the end of the week you have now entered find you still at such a distance from God. Oh, Holy Spirit, return unto thy rest! Deign to make my bosom Thine abode.

Feb. 13th, 1820. . . . May I be taught of God that I may be able to teach others also. It is only the heart that has been deeply exercised in divine things which can enable us to preach experimentally to others. Piety is the life of a minister.[9]

These passages illustrate that piety for Hodge included an experience of feeling on a continuing basis.[10] Obviously he expected his feelings to be affected during a time of worship. Spirituality, therefore, required constant cultivation and involved both the mind and the affections. Piety included at least an ongoing devotional life which served as the presupposed experiential condition of the believer whenever he talked of experimental religion. Worldly thoughts were an intrusion on such a religious life. Hodge's diary reveals his preoccupation with the piety which his friends mention as being so influential on the spiritual lives of others.

Hodge was inaugurated Professor of Oriental and Biblical Literature in 1822. Just prior to his inauguration he married Sarah Bache, and during the next three years the Hodges had three children. Hodge's intention to use the pattern of his own religious upbringing as a pattern for his own children is evidenced in a letter to his mother promising to bring up her grandchildren so that they might be fit for heaven. Drawing, no doubt, from his own childhood he states, "I have great confidence in the effect of religious truth upon the infant mind. Children are so susceptible, their associations are so strong and lasting, that it does not seem strange that the effect of early education should so frequently be felt through life."[11]

Despite his enjoyment of teaching in the seminary, Hodge's sense of the inadequacy of his training in the biblical languages and biblical criticism became an increasing burden to him. In 1826 he decided that for the reputation of the seminary and his own well-being he should spend two years studying in France and Germany under the best scholars in his field. He arranged for a leave of absence from his position, and, having entrusted his family with his mother and brother in Philadelphia, sailed for Europe.

Of great interest are the journal he kept and the letters he exchanged while he was in Europe. From the latter what emerges most clearly is his affection

9. Ibid., pp. 72-74.
10. Ibid., p. 197.
11. Ibid., p. 98.

for his wife and family and for Dr. Alexander. Hodge's letter written after he had seen the Alps for the first time reveals his affection for his wife and the impression that the Alps made on him.

> I have seen the Alps! If now I never see any thing great or beautiful in nature, I am content. I felt that as soon as I saw you, I could fall at your feet and beg you to forgive my beholding such a spectacle without you, my love. You were dearer to me in that moment than ever.[12]

Hodge's description of his impression of the Alps bears a certain resemblance to Alexander's description of the natural bridge in Virginia, which Hodge asserts is far surpassed by the Alps.

> I was walking slowly with my hands behind me, and my eyes on the ground, expecting nothing, when one of the Swiss gentlemen said with infinite indifference—"Viola [sic] les Alpes." I raised my eyes—and around me in a grand amphitheatre, high up against the heavens, were the Alps! It was some moments before the false and indefinite conceptions of my life were overcome by the glorious reality. . . . This was the first moment of my life in which I felt overwhelmed. The natural bridge in Virginia had surprised me—but the first sudden view of the Alps was overwhelming. This was a moment that can never return; the Alps can never be seen again by surprise, and in ignorance of their real appearance.[13]

The other fact that emerges from Hodge's correspondence while in Europe is the almost filial relationship that existed between Hodge and Alexander. In a letter to Alexander from Paris, Hodge expresses the affection he felt for the senior professor at Princeton. Outside his own family Hodge thought of no one with so much affection as he did of Alexander, and there was, he said, "no person excepting my mother to whom I feel so deeply obligated. From my boyhood I have experienced your paternal kindness, and shall cherish as long as I live the recollection of your goodness."[14]

Hodge's journal reveals several incidents in his European stay that are of consequence for his thinking on religious experience. Immediately upon

---

12. Ibid., p. 197.
13. Ibid.
14. Ibid., p. 105. This relationship between the two men continued until Alexander's death in 1851 when he summoned Hodge to his bedside. He gave him a cherished walking stick given to him by one of the chiefs of the Sandwich Islands with the injunction, "You must hand this to your successor in office, that it may be handed down as a kind of symbol of orthodoxy" (LCH, p. 382).

arriving at Halle, Hodge became attached to Dr. F. August Tholuck, one of his professors at the university. They spent hours together in conversation and developed a friendship which was to be lifelong.[15] One of the recurring topics of conversation, since Halle was the traditional hotbed of pietism in the seventeenth century, was the religious situation in Germany. Tholuck confided to Hodge that piety was not encouraged. In fact, he said that "he had much to endure from the many unfounded reports which the enemies of piety were constantly spreading, respecting the few who were of that character here."[16]

It was through Tholuck that Hodge began to understand the thought of Friedrich Schleiermacher, who had been educated by pietists but broken from them in his mature thought. Despite what Hodge considered pantheistic tendencies in his writings, he was obviously impressed that his intimate friend Tholuck owed much of his religious feeling to Schleiermacher's influence. According to Tholuck, Schleiermacher's authority was such that his respect for the Bible and his reverence of Christ exerted a strong influence, without his knowing it, against much speculative thinking. In Tholuck's view the pantheistic philosophy at least led many "to entertain a 'deep religious feeling,' and showed . . . the insufficiency of neological systems."[17] Hodge's journal contains the following comment on Schleiermacher:

> Schleiermacher was originally a moravian and considered very pious and he retains much of the devout spirit which distinguishes that devoted class of men. He often preaches with the greatest fervour and will break out in his family in the hymns written by a pious companion of his earlier years, thus using the language of Christians to give expression to feelings excited by his own peculiar views.[18]

While there might seem to be a touch of criticism in this last remark, it is substantially the same remark made in his *Systematic Theology* when commenting on Schleiermacher's obvious reverence for Christ illustrated in his use of hymns in the church:

> They were always evangelical and spiritual in an eminent degree, filled with praise and gratitude to our Redeemer. Tholuck said that Schleiermacher, when sitting in the evening with his family, would often say,

---

15. Ibid., p. 117.
16. "Journal of European Travels Feb. 1827 - April 1828," p. 19; hereafter "Journal."
17. *LCH*, p. 120.
18. "Journal," p. 13.

"Hush, children; let us sing a hymn of praise to Christ." Can we doubt that he is singing those praises now? To whomsoever Christ is God, St. John assures us, Christ is a Saviour.[19]

Nevertheless, Hodge felt that Schleiermacher had succumbed to the philosophical speculation of the day by allowing it to determine his theology. Hodge always considered it dangerous to mix theology and philosophy, and his general opinion of theological studies in Germany was that they exhibited such a mixture: "It seems to me to be a great misfortune that philosophy is mixed with religion in this country, for it gives so abstruse and mystical character to the explanations of important truths that there is little reason to be surprised that the term mystics has been applied to the advocates of piety."[20] As an example, Hodge notes the tendency to "make faith the development of the life of God in the soul—that is—the divine essence everywhere diffused and the universal agent unfolding itself in the heart."[21] When Tholuck and Hodge discussed this thought, passages from Schleiermacher were consulted and explained by Tholuck which only seemed to "darken counsel by words without wisdom."[22]

Hodge reports one occasion when he heard Schleiermacher preach in Berlin. His comments on the sermon reflect more confusion on Hodge's part than mere disagreement. "The sermon was peculiar. The words were biblical, but the whole tenor so general, the ideas so vague and indefinite, that it was impossible for me to understand exactly what he meant."[23] His opinions of Schleiermacher's thought will be examined in more detail below. Suffice it to say, at this point, that what favorable opinions he had of the great German theologian were due in part to the approving comments of his close friend Tholuck.

In his journal Hodge also describes in great detail his emotional responses during his worship experiences while in Europe. On the occasion of hearing a Rev. Kurtz in Halle he was apparently thrilled at hearing "a real evangelical sermon on Eph. 3:19. . . ." He reports, "My heart overflowed with

---

19. *Systematic Theology*, 2: 440, hereafter ST.
20. "Journal," p. 14.
21. Ibid., pp. 14, 15.
22. Ibid., p. 15. It is interesting that A. A. Hodge in the *LCH* omits certain portions of Hodge's journal including, for instance, the favorable comments on Schleiermacher quoted above and also a disagreement between Hodge and Tholuck on the interpretation of Romans 5, one of the portions staunchly defended by the Princeton men for their position on original sin. The former omission may have been prompted by Hodge's later writings, more critical of Schleiermacher, and the latter by the continuing friendship between Hodge and Tholuck.
23. *LCH*, p. 152.

joy to hear the praise of Christ and the excellence of his love. It has been very long since I have enjoyed so much pleasure in hearing a sermon. For here, there are few who appear to feel the spirit of the gospel or whose hearts are warmed with the love of the blessed Saviour. God bless Kurtz."[24] His reaction was much the same when he attended a communion service in a correctional institution for boys in Berlin. After recounting the service, Hodge adds an introspective comment.

> I have recently been more than ever, I think, affected by a sense of the indescribable excellence of our adorable Saviour, his character has appeared to me in a purity and beauty which my blind eyes have been long in discovering. Oh that I should see more of this loveliness everyday that I live and be more transformed into his image.[25]

He was not without reactions toward the other extreme, however. When he attended a Good Friday service in a Lutheran church in Berlin, the service closely resembled a Catholic mass. When communion was celebrated the worshipers went to two clergyman and were not permitted to touch the elements. Hodge commented: "I felt like a stranger here, and longed for the time when again, in the simple Scriptural manner of our church I could partake of the memorials of our dying Saviour's love."[26] His strongest reaction was in the city of Jena. He states that he heard two "miserably cold anti-christian sermons. . . ." Indeed, he was nowhere else "so strongly impressed with the total absence of religion. I am told [he recounts] that the students boast of the fact that they have nothing of fanaticism among them."[27]

When Hodge was in Berlin he received several reports of revival which broke out in Pomerania. The first was a generally favorable report of the work of a small family which resulted in up to 600 people meeting in private houses despite opposition by both civil and ecclesiastical authorities. On another occasion Hodge heard stories of "demoniacal possession" concerning a woman who was supposed to have "rolled over and over" and have her mind thrown into a state resembling "ecstasy." In this state she "would prophesy (in what sense of that word I know not)." When the woman was

---

24. "Journal," p. 22.
25. Ibid., p. 93. On still another occasion Hodge tells of his being much moved simply from hearing an effective use of an organ accompanied by four trumpets in a confirmation service. "This is the first time I have heard this kind of music in a church. The effect upon my feelings was very strong and very pleasing" ("Journal," p. 25).
26. Ibid., p. 32.
27. Ibid., p. 73.

not in such a state, she was reported to be a "true, humble Christian."[28] It is obvious that young Hodge did not know what to make of such reports. He did, however, draw a comparison between this revival and phenomena in America.

> It is certainly remarkable that on both sides of the Atlantic seasons of religious excitement should be attended by such similar outward appearances—whether the people under such influence in our country said that they saw visions or not I do not know—that was the case here. Is it anything like . . . the New Testament?[29]

Later in his career Hodge would never have asked this question as he increasingly opposed Finney's revivals. Nevertheless, under the influence of Tholuck, Hodge expressed a favorable reaction to revivalistic phenomena.

Further evidence of Hodge's capacity for and expression of feeling is found in references to his family life. The deep affection he expressed for his mother and his wife he also communicated to other members of his family. Hodge's son noted in *The Life of Charles Hodge* that the study in the Hodge home had two doors, one opening toward the seminary for students to use and the other opening into the main hall of the house. Thus the whole family had easy access to the father. Hodge removed the latches from the door and put springs on them so that even the smallest member of the family could enter at will. The younger Hodge said of the family worship that his father prayed for the members gathered about his knees "with such soul-felt tenderness, that however bad we were our hearts all melted to his touch." In fact it was the private family life that the children most remembered: "That which makes those days sacred in the retrospect of his children is the person and character of the father himself . . . all radiant as that was with love, with unwavering faith, and with unclouded hope."[30] He goes on to say that although his father's talents in music were not exceptional, he loved good music. He especially loved singing hymns "which appealed to the religious affections. The children remembered his singing devotional hymns while pacing in his study.[31]

The depth of Hodge's emotional nature is most easily seen in his reaction to his wife's death in 1845. In his "Memoranda," a daily record of weather

28. Ibid., p. 101.
29. Ibid., p. 102.
30. *LCH*, p. 227.
31. Ibid.

conditions along with other miscellaneous notes, sayings, and records, Hodge recorded their last conversation. He asked her, "Do you love the Lord Jesus? . . . Do you trust him?" to which she answered "I hope so" and "Entirely." When he asked, "Is he precious to you?" she replied, "Very. . . . He is my all in all." Following the report of her death on Christmas day, Hodge penned a deeply affectionate note in his record book.

> Blesst saint; companion of my boyhood—my first and only love—my most devoted wife—mother of my children—all sacred memories cluster around you; and all who knew you pronounce you blessed. May the God of infinite mercy send the Holy Spirit to take in this family your place, and be the instructor, guide and comforter of your household and bring all your children to a life of devotion to the Lord Jesus.[32]

His memory of her was such that after each Sunday following her death he numbered the day—i.e., "first Sunday after," "second Sunday after," etc. He noted the first time he preached after her death. The practice of numbering Sundays continues for 132 weeks. After September 16, 1857, he recorded it was the anniversary of the last time she heard him preach. He placed a thick black line beside each December 25th from the time of her death until 1854.

This section has included more than references to Hodge's personal religious life in order to bring in his specific comments on religious trends while he was in Europe. These comments are not peripheral to the main issue of this study. His reaction, for instance, to Schleiermacher and the Pomeranian revivals reveal his early thinking relating to matters of religious experience. His statements subsequent to hearing Schleiermacher's preaching, for example, are more than an intellectual judgment. That instance, combined with his comments on the Lutheran communion service, reveals the kind of worship experience to which he was most accustomed—i.e., clear sermons with doctrinal exposition.

The similarities and contrasts between Hodge's and Alexander's personal religious lives are quite evident. While both were raised in Presbyterian homes, Alexander had a close association with revivalism. He had what he considered to be both good and bad experiences through this association. Previous to this exposure his life was virtually devoid of any kind of piety. He had simply learned the catechism as a memory lesson. The boyhood religious experiences of Hodge, however, formed the central part of his life.

---

32. "Memoranda," vol. 2, entry for Dec. 25, 1849.

Piety and devotion were cultivated from his childhood, and the religious life of his youth was only deepened in later life. This is not to say that his conversion experience was not identical to Alexander's. Both would have called theirs a valid experience of regeneration. But Hodge's certainly was not as outwardly dramatic. Hodge had no continuing association with the kind of revivalism that Alexander did. In fact, he tended more to deprecate revivals than did his predecessor. Nevertheless, an openness is clearly evident at times, as the thought at least occurred to Hodge that perhaps the phenomena of the Pomeranian revivals might be analogous to certain New Testament phenomena, giving them a certain sanction.[33] As will be obvious from the discussion below on Hodge's later appraisal of such phenomena, his opinions were to change decidedly.

The diaries kept by the two men are similar in content but differ in degree. Both are the records of their religious feelings and experiences connected with their preaching. While Alexander's reflects the intensity of a revivalistic environment, Hodge's is more subdued. Perhaps this is due in part to Alexander's discouraging the keeping of spiritual journals. Nevertheless, both indicate the practical importance attributed to their religious feelings. The journals almost functioned as spiritual barometers indicating a good or bad spiritual state. To continue the analogy of the barometer, the two men seem to have had more spiritual "lows" than "highs." Such spiritual struggles were congruent with their emphasis on the necessity of discipline and effort in the Christian life and the difficulty of maintaining a good spiritual warfare.

When we compare their experiences, it is evident that Hodge profited from the close association with his friend. Alexander obviously had no control over Hodge's early religious experiences, and yet, parenthetically, they reflect in a noteworthy way what Alexander had to say in his *Thoughts on Religious Experience* concerning the religious experiences of children.[34] Of much greater significance is the lack of emotional excesses in Hodge's journal, such as the excesses Alexander had found so troubling in his life. Hodge expresses deep concern for the state of his affections to the extent that it is the sole subject discussed in the journal. But Hodge seems to

---

33. Although Hodge did not identify what New Testament phenomena he meant, it is a safe conjecture that he had in mind the visions, revelations, and prophecies mentioned in the Book of Acts and the Pauline Epistles.

34. A study of chapter 2 in Alexander's *Thoughts on Religious Experience* reveals similarities between Alexander's views on piety in childhood and Hodge's religious experiences mentioned above.

have avoided especially the almost morbid introspection so evident with Alexander. Both men appear to have the same concern for their devotional lives. They openly expressed their emotions in their private devotions. The introduction to Alexander's hymnal was exemplified in Hodge's predilection for hymns appealing to the religious affections. Thus while neither was given to dismissing his private religious experience, the existing evidence points to a definite similarity in their emotional content and the priority given to such practices.

Hodge's Systematic Writings

Several studies have been devoted either wholly or in part to explicating and evaluating Hodge's three-volume *Systematic Theology*. The study that has dealt in some measure with the subject of religious experience in Hodge's thought is the unpublished Ph.D. thesis of James L. McAllister: "The Nature of Religious Knowledge in the Theology of Charles Hodge." McAllister traces in great detail what was noted in the first chapter concerning the philosophical strain that appears throughout the Princeton theology. He examines the thought of the Scottish philosopher 'Thomas Reid and shows the significant influence that Reid's philosophy has in Hodge's epistemology. What can be noted in Hodge owing to his dependence on Scottish philosophy, according to McAllister, is an empiricism, rationalism, dualism, and implicit authoritarianism. In the duality between subject and object, both of which are created by God, the perceiving subject is so constituted that the reason begins with external senses and in an inductive manner gathers facts. Certain intuitive principles are assumed, one of the most important being that the mind is so constituted that whether it perceives the material world, cause and effect, or truth and error, it correctly perceives what is. Reason judges between evidences that are presented to it. Both natural knowledge and the knowledge of faith are based on evidence presented to the mind. The implicit authoritarianism is evident in Hodge's frequent appeals to the assumed first principles of common sense realism, which he substantiates not by rational arguments but by appeal to the universal acceptance of them by people of all nations and ages.[35]

---

35. James L. McAllister, "The Nature of Religious Knowledge in the Theology of Charles Hodge," pp. 67-122. Besides McAllister's and John O. Nelson's thesis mentioned above, the following studies, which include evaluations of Hodge's work, should be mentioned: Penrose St. Amant, "The Rise and Early Development of the Princeton School of Theology,"

McAllister's thesis is valuable as an exposition of Hodge's dependence on the Scottish philosophy. This is a critical point since Hodge continued the two-front attack begun by Alexander against speculative philosophy, on the one hand, and those who were more subjective, on the other. But in his *Systematic Theology* Hodge directs his opposition in a slightly revised form. The opening chapters on method contain the outlines of not only his methodology but also his criticism of rationalism and mysticism. Hodge begins by claiming that theology is a science. The Bible, while not a system of theology, provides the facts, the raw data, by which a system of theology is constructed by the inductive method. The inductive is one of the three methods that have been used in theological formulation, the other two being the speculative and the mystical methods.

The speculative method assumes certain *a priori* principles and from them deduces what is and must be. The three general forms of the speculative method are the deistic and rationalistic form, the dogmatic form, and the transcendentalist form. Deistical rationalism denies that any source of knowledge of divine things exists other than what can be found in nature and in the constitution of the mind. Deists repudiate supernatural revelation in any form, whether it be in the form of Scripture or interference in the forces of nature. They assume certain metaphysical and moral axioms that provide the basis for all other truth deduced from them. The dogmatic form assumes a supernatural divine revelation, but this is reduced to some philosophical system. Some of the Fathers substituted γνῶσις for πίστις, and even Anselm succumbed to the dogmatic form. Whenever this form has been prevalent, rational evidence and knowledge take precedence over the Bible and faith. Finally, the transcendentalist form assumes no divine revelation but contends that truth is found in man and the historical development of the human race. Truth is discovered by a process of thought.[36]

On the other hand the mystical method, according to Hodge, is antithetical to the speculative. Whereas speculation depends on a process of thought, mysticism involves only the feelings. As to method in theology, mysticism has been both supernatural and natural. In supernatural mysticism either

unpublished Ph.D. thesis (University of Edinburgh, 1952); William D. Livingston's, "The Princeton Apologetic as Exemplified by the Work of Benjamin B. Warfield and J. Gresham Machen," unpublished Ph.D. thesis (Yale, 1948); and Earl A. Pope, "New England Calvinism and the Disruption in the Presbyterian Church," unpublished Ph.D. thesis (Brown, 1962).

36. *ST*, I: 4-6. Hodge mentions no deistic rationalists by name. The most contemporary of dogmatic rationalists cited specifically is Christian Wolf, who died in 1754. As for the transcendentalists he identifies only Europeans such as Karl Daub and Rosenkranz.

God or God's Spirit has direct communion with an individual soul. It assumes that "God by his immediate intercourse with the soul, reveals through the feelings and by means . . . of intuitions, divine truth independently of the outward teaching of his Word."[37] Hodge contends that all Christians are mystics in the sense that the Holy Spirit illuminates minds of believers so that they have knowledge of the truths objectively revealed in the Scriptures. In fact, he states that some Christians have been called mystics when all they were advocating was the inward teaching of the Holy Spirit. However, once it is assumed that the Spirit reveals new truths not already given in the Scriptures in such a way that the Spirit is to be followed to the neglect of the Scriptures, mysticism is not Christian.

A second form of mysticism is natural. In this form it is not God but man's natural religious consciousness that is the source of religious knowledge. Religious feelings are the vehicle of truth differing only in degree from person to person. Since all men have a religious nature, everyone more or less clearly apprehends religious truth. The religious consciousness is conditioned by various influences that affect it. With the appearance of Christ the influence was great and has been retained as people's feelings have been affected by His influence. The consequences of the mystical methodology are carefully noted by Hodge. First the meaning of the terms "revelation" and "inspiration" are greatly devalued. They become not the objective presentation of truth to the mind in the case of the former or the supernatural guidance of the Spirit enabling the believer to communicate infallibly truth to others in the latter. Rather, are they common to all men in various degrees even to the present. Secondly, the Bible as the authoritative record of God's revelation is depreciated. It is assumed to be culturally conditioned and bears marks of its time which render it incapable of universal authority in matters of doctrine. Mystical method transforms Christianity so that it is no longer a system of doctrine. "It is a life, an influence, a subjective state; or by whatever term it may be expressed or explained, it is a power within each individual Christian determining his feelings and his views of divine things."[38] A corollary of this is that a Christian theologian, rather than interpreting the doctrine of the Scripture, simply explicates his religious consciousness. Schleiermacher's *Glaubenslehre* is the most significant instance of this natural mystical methodology.[39]

37. Ibid., p. 7.
38. Ibid., pp. 8, 9. Hodge did not deny Christianity can be defined as a life, but he denied that it can be restricted to that. Cf. below for Hodge's complete definition of Christianity.
39. Ibid., p. 9.

Hodge proposes an inductive approach in theology to combat the errors of rationalism and mysticism. The theologian presupposes certain laws God has impressed upon man's nature. He assumes that the senses are trustworthy as are men's mental operations, and that cause and effect are real. The theologian then proceeds to gather facts from the Bible just as the natural scientist gathers facts from nature. What is most important is that while the works of God, the constitution of man's nature, and the religious experience of believers encompass the truths with which the theologian deals, the Scriptures always authenticate these truths. Therefore, to preclude the possibility of false inference either from the works of God in nature or from one's religious consciousness and the laws of man's nature, the Scriptures contain everything that can be learned from these sources.[40] Otherwise, the various intuitions of man would give rise to myriad theologies.

To counteract the possibility that men will reason wrongly, Hodge insisted on the importance of the testimony of the Holy Spirit in his chapter on method. Without the inward teaching of the Holy Spirit, which gives rise to saving faith based on the Spirit's testimony and demonstration of the truth, Christian theology would differ from theologian to theologian. Two facts regarding the Spirit's testimony are of utmost importance: (1) The teaching of the Spirit is limited to truths already found in the Scriptures. No revelation of new truth is involved, only an illumination of the mind to truths already given. (2) Valid Christian experience is depicted in the Scriptures. Not only are the facts included regarding God and Christ and the plan of salvation but also the effects these facts produce in the life of the believer, with the result that "we cannot appeal to our own feelings or inward experience, as a ground or guide, unless we can show that it agrees with the experience of holy men as recorded in the Scriptures."[41]

Then Hodge outlines how the Spirit's inner teaching relates to a theologian's task. Following Augustine, Calvin, and the Genevan theologians, Hodge accords the teaching of the Spirit a place in the theologians writing theology even though it is no substitute for revelation itself. Subjectively considered, the question for the theologian becomes not "what is true to the understanding but what is true to the renewed heart?"[42] Christian theologians attempt not to align the Bible with speculative philosophy but to subject their thoughts to the truth of God as it is mediated by the Spirit to the

40. Ibid., p. 11.
41. Ibid., p. 16.
42. Ibid.

heart. Hodge's comprehensive statement, therefore, is the following:

> The true method in theology requires that the facts of religious experi-
> ence should be accepted as facts, and when duly authenticated by
> Scripture, be allowed to interpret the doctrinal statements of the Word
> of God. So legitimate and powerful is this inward teaching of the Spirit,
> that it is no uncommon thing to find men having two theologies,—one
> of the intellect, and another of the heart. The one may find expression in
> creeds and systems of divinity: the other in their prayers and hymns. It
> would be safe for a man to resolve to admit into his theology nothing
> which is not sustained by the devotional writings of true Christians of
> every denomination.[43]

The important point to remember, however, is that the two theologies, while
distinguished from each other, do not differ. Despite the diversity of their
manifestations in creeds and prayers, they are not different in essence. This
was Hodge's main point in a series of articles he wrote in the *Biblical
Repertory* in a controversy with E. A. Park, a professor in Andover Theological Seminary. Hodge understands Park to say that a theology of the intellect
is "understood by logical consciousness," and theology of the feeling is
"felt by intuitional consciousness," and that the two do not necessarily
agree. While the former is well suited for rational analysis and logical
defense, the latter is not so fitted.

Hodge admits that certain figurative passages of Scripture are to be
interpreted differently than literal passages are. Nevertheless, the figurative
passages in his opinion connote something just as definite. To say that God is
our shepherd presents a definite idea to the mind despite the fact that it is
different from other more literal statements.

> Such language, when interpreted according to established usage, and
> made to mean what it was intended to express, is not only definite in its
> import, but it never expresses what is false to the intellect. The feelings
> demand truth in their object; and no utterance is as natural or effective as
> the language of the emotion, which does not satisfy the under-
> standing.[44]

---

43. Ibid., pp. 16, 17.
44. "Theology of the Intellect and that of the Feelings," *Biblical Repertory and Princeton
Review*, 22, no. 4 (1850): 652. The complementary relation between the two theologies is
analogous to C. S. Lewis's epistemology. Lewis posits a dialectical relationship between
reason and imagination. Cf. Richard B. Cunningham, *C. S. Lewis: Defender of the Faith*
(Philadelphia, The Westminster Press), 1967, and W. Andrew Hoffecker and John Tim-
merman, "Watchmen in the City: C. S. Lewis's View of Male and Female," *The Cresset*, 41
(Valparaiso Univ. Press, 1978): 4.

Scriptural statements that God repents or is jealous or even that He has wings under which His people find comfort are true to the feelings but are just as true in a different sense to the understanding. If they were not true in some sense to the understanding, they could not be true to the feelings.

> It is because calling God our shepherd presents the idea of a person exercising a kind care over us, that it has power to move the affections. If it presented any conception inconsistent with the truth it would grate on the feelings as much as it would offend the intellect.[45]

Hodge concludes that both a theology of the intellect and a theology of the feeling must be true, otherwise no one would believe them. Because Christians agree so frequently in their inward experience of doctrine, they are more easily united in their hymns, liturgies, and devotions than they are in their creedal statements.

What is significant about Hodge's argument is that it echoes exactly what Alexander argued in his article about certain Baptists and their feelings about close communion. A believer's theology of the intellect may need correction from his theology of the feelings. The theology of the intellect is more likely to be faulty than his theology of the feelings. This does not mean that differences in doctrinal professions are matters of small importance. But it does mean that one can ascertain the real faith of people more clearly and uniformly in their hymns and expressions of devotion than in their creeds and theologies. If this is true, then it could not be assumed that the theology of the feelings is false. This is especially evident when one considers that Hodge, in agreement with Alexander, stated that the religious feelings one has are the result of the Holy Spirit's working in the heart along with the objective truth found in the Scriptures. The feelings are the "necessary attributes of spiritual cognition." Again he dispels any hint that this is "the light system," i.e., simply a mechanical operation or a stimulus-response mechanism by which "the heart is changed by the mere objective presentation of the truth."[46] The operation of the Holy Spirit is the means by which the soul is regenerated. The Holy Spirit so works that the believer's experience always mirrors what is depicted in the Scriptures as true Christian experience.

This is amply illustrated by tracing references in the *Systematic Theology* wherein Hodge, in discussing various doctrines, appeals to the religious

---

45. "'Theology of the Intellect and that of the Feelings," p. 652.
46. Ibid., p. 672.

experience of believers as an evidence of their truth. In the section on originals in Hodge appeals to the universal consent of the church as evidence of the work of the Holy Spirit working through the Word and in the hearts of believers. In doing so, he appeals not so much to the decisions of church councils as might be expected. Rather he appeals to the "formulas of devotion," which come from the people.

> It is, as often remarked, in the prayers, in the hymnology; in the devotional writings which true believers make the channel of their communion with God, and the medium through which they express their most intimate religious convictions that we must look for the universal faith. [The doctrine of original sin] pervades the prayers, the worship, and the institutions of the Church.[47]

Hodge uses essentially the same argument when discussing the atoning work of Christ. Christians have expressed their relation to Christ by using such biblical terms as sacrifice, ransom, and propitiation. The feelings that have been expressed in liturgies, prayers, hymns, and devotional diaries all point to an acceptance of the biblical view of Christ's substitutionary atonement. He cites several verses from hymns, such as:

> Jesus, my God, Thy blood alone hath power
> sufficient to atone

and

> My soul looks back to see the burdens Thou
> didst bear,
> When hanging on the cursed tree, and hopes
> her sins were there.

Hodge asks rhetorically, "Does any Christian refuse to sing such hymns? Do they not express his inmost religious convictions? If they do not agree with the speculations of his understanding, do they not express the feelings of his heart and the necessities of his fallen nature?"[48] Hodge contends that other theories that teach the atonement as simply didactic or exemplary fail in two points. They fail to provide for expiation of sin and an answer for a guilty conscience, and secondly, they "do not account for the intimate personal relation between Christ and the believer which is everywhere recognized in the Scripture, and which is so precious in the view of all true Christians."[49] He insists that the New Testament represents Christ as "the

47. *ST*, II, p. 250.
48. Ibid., p. 525.
49. Ibid., pp. 525, 526.

immediate and constant source of life and of all good."[50]

Hodge's theology, therefore, is consistent with his methodology. As in the case of Alexander the Scriptures are the ultimate court of appeal. They not only prescribe the doctrines of the Christian faith but also explicitly outline the experience which attends belief. Because believers are still fallible, this may prohibit a correct intellectual interpretation of the Scriptures. In such cases, it may be necessary to turn to the hymns, liturgies, and devotional writings Christians have written throughout the course of church history as reflections of their Christian experiences. These writings not only exhibit a remarkable unanimity but are in the most profound sense thoroughly biblical in their perspective. Both Hodge and Alexander saw the necessity of the Scriptures as a norm for experience, and both appealed to the experience of believers as corroborating the external authority of the Bible.[51] In the final analysis, from a practical standpoint, Hodge has a high place for experience in the determination and corroboration of Christian theology.

The reason for Hodge's relatively strong critique of experience in some contexts was his response to several religious trends. Revivalism was a continuing concern to the Princeton men and Hodge's evaluation will be treated below. But what concerned him most in his *Systematic Theology* was the growing acceptance of Schleiermacher's method. For Hodge it exhibited "mystical" traits. While all Christians can be called mystics because they stress the supernatural influence of the Holy Spirit, Hodge means by "mystical" those who stress immediacy and passivity in experience and who stress mystical communion with God at the expense of the ordinary means of grace such as the Word and sacraments.

But a wider use of "mysticism" includes any system that stresses the feelings above the intellect. In Hodge's opinion Schleiermacher has misunderstood what Christianity is from both an objective and a subjective point of view. Because he posited Christianity as a function of one's feelings or dependence upon God, and had redefined revelation and inspiration in light of a reinterpretation of Christianity's essence, Christianity subjectively considered is reduced to "the intentions of good men, as occasioned and determined by the appearance of Christ." But more importantly, objectively

---

50. Ibid., p. 526.

51. Ibid. Hodge appeals to the experience of believers in several other instances as proof for doctrines: inability (p. 271), free agency (p. 303), sovereignty of the Spirit (p. 344), work of the Spirit and the Word (p. 664), efficacious grace (p. 706).

considered Christian theology is "the logical analysis, and scientific arrangement and elucidation of the truths involved in those intuitions."[52] The Scriptures in such a method are devoid of any significant authority, important only as the first record of the awakening to religious consciousness of the apostles. Feelings usurp the role of God's Word.

Hodge's most succinct answer to Schleiermacher's subjective method appears in an article "What is Christianity?" In it he defined Christianity from two perspectives.

> Christianity is both a doctrine and a life, and . . . the object of true faith is both a proposition and a person. . . . Christianity objectively considered, is the testimony of God concerning his son, it is the whole revelation of truth contained in the Scriptures, concerning the redemption of man through Jesus Christ our Lord. Subjectively considered, it is the life of Christ in the soul, or, that form of spiritual life which has its origin in Christ, is determined by the revelation concerning his person and work, which is due to the indwelling of his Spirit.[53]

By this statement regarding the objective and subjective Hodge made explicit what was implicit in all of Alexander's writings. Although Alexander never used the two terms, they capture his ideas on the nature of Christian belief. Only this definition makes intelligible the deeply emotional religious experiences of both Alexander and Hodge. That Christianity was an experience of grace manifested in peace and joy did not preclude their saying that Christianity is also the Scriptures and statements of doctrine. The converse of this is also true. Hodge's summary definition is a reaction against what he considered to be Schleiermacher's and his followers' elimination of "Christianity objectively considered." Hodge countered Schleiermacher's reinterpretation through omission by emphasizing to a greater degree the necessity of the objective element in Christian faith. Hodge contended that while it would be incorrect to separate the objective and subjective elements in Christianity, it would be error compounded either to exclude the objective completely or to put the subjective elements in the prominent position.[54]

Hodge substantiated his view that subjective experience should be based

---

52. Ibid., I, p. 66.
53. "What is Christianity?" *Biblical Repertory and Princeton Review*, 33, no. 1 (1860): 119.
54. Hodge also opposed the Quakers in their employment of mystical methodology. Their doctrine of the Spirit was inherited from mysticism. He distinguished the Princeton notion of the Spirit's illumination from the Quaker's inner light because the inner light in the Quaker view tends to supersede the authority of the Scripture (*ST*, I, pp. 102, 103).

on the objective element of Christianity with a detailed analysis of faith. His discussion builds on Alexander's previous work. Faith consists of two elements: assent and trust. McAllister characterizes Hodge's view as intellectualistic.[55] While Hodge makes assent precede trust and includes subtle distinctions, trust is firmly asserted. Hodge carefully demonstrates the association between trust and the acceptance of something as trustworthy: "To regard a thing as true, is to regard it as worthy of trust, as being what it purports to be."[56]

But faith is not limited to a bare intellectual assent to something as true. Saving faith in Christ involves both assent and trust.

> When we are commanded to believe in Christ as the Savior of men, we are not required merely to assent to the proposition that he does save sinners, but also to receive and rest upon Him alone for our own salvation.[57]

Saving faith, therefore, is more than a mere act of the mind. It incorporates several of man's faculties: the understanding, the heart, and the will. Believing in Christ is synonymous with receiving Christ and resting in him for salvation. Therefore, by defining faith as knowledge, Hodge's intention was not to intellectualize it, but to protect it from mystical interpretations. While McAllister's criticism has some substance, Hodge has far from neglected the subjective elements of trust and personal relationship with God.

Not all of Hodge's writings were cast in the same intellectual mold of his *Systematic Theology*. He wrote *The Way of Life* at the request of the American Sunday School Union so that it might be used by "intelligent and educated young persons, either to arouse their attention, or to guide their steps in the WAY OF LIFE."[58] We might well characterize this volume as a miniature or layman's edition of his *Systematic Theology*. Specifically it was to deal with the three questions of whether the Scriptures are a revelation from God, and if they are, what their teaching was, and what effect these doctrines are to have on the heart.

Hodge begins the first chapter by treating the internal evidences for the divine origin of the Scriptures. He asserts unequivocally "no amount of

---

55. McAllister, op. cit., p. 274.
56. *ST*, III, p. 43.
57. Ibid., p. 91.
58. *The Way of Life*, pp. v, vi.

mere external evidence can produce genuine faith."[59] The fault lay not in the external evidence but in the moral state of the heart. But the most important of the evidences is not the external but the internal. In the internal evidences of the Scripture the believer perceives the impress of God because the internal evidences are not primarily intellectual in nature. They are moral. Internal evidence therefore is not restricted to an intellectual elite but is open even to a child. Negatively, internal evidence consists in the absence from the Scripture of anything incompatible with a divine origin. Positively it bears the marks of God: "There is in the word of God, and especially in the person and character of Jesus Christ, a clear and wonderful manifestation of the divine glory."[60] When one reads the scriptural accounts of Christ and the demands that are made with regard to worship and morals, it is clear that biblical faith does not depend on external evidence that fails to impinge on a person's moral nature. Since the Scripture makes demands on us by its very content, it is evident that it bears the impress of the divine.

The writers of Scripture clearly teach such a view. Although appeal was often made to signs, miracles, and the gifts of the Spirit as confirming what they taught (external evidences), their most common appeal was to the manifestation of the truth *in* what they taught and did. Hodge concludes: "It is, therefore, plainly the doctrine of the authority or command of God manifesting itself therein, in a manner analogous to the exhibition of his perfections in the works of nature."[61] Hodge's argument for internal evidences then is an argument from experience, the experience of God's truth perceived in the reading of Scripture.

Hodge used this argument as well. Even though one of the other sources is a sermon, it will be mentioned at this juncture because it bears so directly on the point under consideration. In "The Place of the Bible in a System of Education" Hodge underscores the importance of instruction in the Scriptures. The Bible communicates knowledge that includes certain historical and biographical details. It contains instructive parables and general principles for moral action. But the Scriptures do more than give information. While at one instance they might be "reasoning with men in a manner to tax all their powers, at another [they might be] addressing them in such strains of sublimity or beauty, as to waken up all the finer feelings of the soul."[62]

---

59. Ibid., p. 14.
60. Ibid., p. 29.
61. Ibid., pp. 34-35.
62. "The Place of the Bible in a System of Education," p. 7.

Reading the content of the Bible establishes the optimum situation for the generation of a true faith because the Bible contains elements that appeal to both the intellect and the heart. "In the Bible we find truth, adapted at once to enlarge the intellect and purify the heart. The idea of God, in the infinitude of his perfections cannot enter the mind without expanding its capacities, while it sheds into the inmost recesses of the soul its sanctifying influences."[63] Turning to the figure of Christ, Hodge notes that Christianity is as much indebted for its attractiveness to the superhuman loveliness of [Christ's] character . . . as to any one of its doctrines. There is in this faultless model of human excellence, a moral power which few are able to resist."[64] Especially is this true in the case of children. If people would have their children confronted with Christ in the Bible, they would be exposing them to a more positive moral influence than all the systems of morals ever devised.

To conclude his section on internal evidences in *The Way of Life* Hodge appealed to the experience of many Christians who, if asked why they believed in the Bible, would be unable to give a detailed answer. Such people, contends Hodge, while not able to give a detailed explanation, do not believe simply because others do or because someone has sufficiently demonstrated in a deductive manner the Bible's divine origin. Such people instead believe for substantially the same reason they believe in God, "and they believe in God because they see his glory and feel his authority and power."[65]

What is significant in the remainder of *The Way of Life* is the way in which Hodge illustrates the effects of the cardinal doctrines of Christianity on the feelings of believers. Hodge's description of the effect of the doctrine of justification on the feelings is a prime example of the way in which he conceived the relation between the objective and subjective aspects in Christian experience. Man needs to be justified in the sight of God because he has disobeyed God's law. God has not left man without a means of salvation, however, and has provided a plan of salvation. This plan is that God justifies man by grace through faith in the work of Christ. Christ's righteousness is imputed to man who is unrighteous. As a result man experiences peace with God.

Peace, therefore, is not the result of the assurance of mere pardon, but of

63. Ibid., p. 9.
64. Ibid., p. 10.
65. Hodge, op. cit., p. 35.

pardon founded upon a righteousness which illustrates the character of God, which magnifies the law and makes it honourable; which satisfies the justice of God, while it displays the infinite riches of his tenderness and love.[66]

The doctrine of justification by faith presents faith as the only method by which men are delivered from sin. Before they are justified they feel themselves to be sinners and under the condemnation of the law's demands. They feel as if they are unreconciled to God. In such a state they do not have the experience of real love and peace.

> But when they are brought to see that God, through his infinite love has set forth Jesus Christ as a propitiation for our sins . . . that it is not by works of righteousness which we have done, but according to his mercy he saveth us; they are emancipated from their former bondage and made the sons of God. . . . The whole relation of the soul to God is changed, and all our feelings and conduct change with it. . . . Till then we were slaves and enemies, and have the feelings of slaves. When we have accepted the terms of reconciliation we are the sons of God and have the feelings of sons.[67]

The subjective feeling of the individual is in exact dependence upon his objective position *vis-à-vis* God. When a person is not justified, he feels condemned and feels that he is indeed not reconciled to God. To claim that he has peace and joy and feels like a reconciled son of God would be only a product of his imagination and not the result of an objective reconciliation, justification, and forgiveness. Pardon and forgiveness, which result in peace, are not some vain figments of the imagination, feelings to be called up at one's command. Peace, joy, and the feelings of being a son of God are the product of an objective reality. If a person is not in fact reconciled, there is no basis on which he can feel peace. The reconciliation must take place prior to the experience otherwise one is deluding himself with a false sense of security. Here is the heart of Hodge's argument against any subjectivist theology wherein the ultimate appeal of certainty is to one's feelings rather than to the work of Christ.

In the latter part of *The Way of Life* Hodge discusses the profession of religion, holy living, and the process of sanctification. The role of the feelings is prominent in each of these areas of the outward duties of religion. Our feelings, now regenerate, instructively influence us to undertake them.

---

66. Ibid., p. 209.
67. Ibid., pp. 210-11.

Brotherly love, worship, and prayer are duties that renewed hearts find delight in doing. The motive to obedience is not "mere regard to authority."[68]

Sanctification

In defining religious life Hodge contends that progress should characterize the Christian life. True religion is therefore to be defined as

> not an external service; nor is it a mere excitement of fear and sorrow succeeded by peace and joy; nor is it a fitful alternation of such exercises. It is a permanent principle of action, spontaneous in its exercises and progressive in its nature. . . . It is a participation of the divine nature, or the conformity of the soul to God.[69]

This may be restated simply as knowledge of God. He means knowledge in its broadest sense for it is a knowledge not only of perception and recognition but also of approbation that enlarges knowledge beyond its merely cognitive connotation. Hodge contends that the whole man is affected—the mind is enlightened, the will is aligned with the purpose of God, and the affections are purified. He actually states that the idea is for a "symmetrical development" of the various faculties.[70]

When Hodge expands on the nature of this spiritual knowledge he explains it as communion with a personal God. He leads into this discussion by noting that the Christian experiences love for the divine perfections. But he wants to say more than this, for the believer not only loves the divine attributes but enters into a love of personal communion. "It is the love of a personal being, who stands in the most intimate relations to ourselves . . . as our father, who with conscious love watches over us . . . [and] holds communion with us."[71] Hodge describes this relationship as either brief or more prolonged in duration depending on whether thoughts of God are fleeting or diligently sought in a kind of retreat from the world.

> The spirit of devotion which so preeminently distinguished the Redeemer, dwells in all his people. They are all devout; they all walk with God; they all feel him to be near and rejoice in his presence; and they all have communion with him in acts of private and public worship.[72]

Then Hodge returns to the symmetrical image by saying that God in His providence ensures that as the spiritual life progresses, the individual finds

68. Ibid., p. 282.
69. Ibid., pp. 334-35.
70. Ibid., p. 338.
71. Ibid., p. 340.
72. Ibid., pp. 341-42.

the exercises of the soul are attended proportionately by peace and joy. Whereas the sensible impressions, the social affections, the intellectual powers, and the moral emotions form an ascending ladder of pleasure, the highest of pleasures are those of the religious affections. Therefore, communion with God is the highest of pleasures. Joy and peace result.

> Joy, therefore is one of the fruits of the Spirit; it is one of the accompaniments and evidences of spiritual life; it is a healthful affusion; it is the oil of gladness, which the Spirit pours over the renewed soul, to invigorate its exercises, to brighten its visage, and to make it active in the service and praise of God.[73]

Such description is reminiscent of Alexander's description of the religious life. Religious life is generated by union of the believer with Christ and participation in the life of Christ is effected by the believer's partaking of the Holy Spirit. But when it comes to explaining the union, Hodge simply asserts that it is mysterious. Through prayer the believer communicates with the Holy Spirit and such communications are the means "by which the life of God in the soul is maintained and promoted."[74] As to specific things the Christian can do to cultivate the spiritual life, contemplation of truth, worship, and performance of duty are encouraged with the emphasis being on the subject's putting truths before the mind rather than communing with God. Hodge quotes Scripture verses which emphasize the sanctifying power of the Bible, the necessity of worship, and the value of doing good. Only when he deals with worship does he mention the element of communion with God. But it includes only the following assertion with no discussion as to the nature of the communion or of the receiving of God's communications:

> It [worship] not only includes the exercise and expression of all pious feelings, which are necessarily strengthened by the exercise, but it is the appointed means of holding communion with God and receiving the communications of his grace.[75]

We will find in Hodge's devotional writings a greater elaboration on the nature of this communion with God. However, in his systematic writings Hodge simply states that such experiences are common to Christians without explaining their exact nature.

In these formal writings it seems apparent that although Hodge has essentially taken up the attack begun by Alexander on two fronts, the

---

73. Ibid., p. 345.
74. Ibid., p. 374.
75. Ibid., p. 377.

speculative or rationalistic approach to religion on the one hand and the mystical approach on the other, the latter has emerged as the more auspicious foe in the guise of subjectivism. Hodge did not wholly ignore the rationalistic methodology—part of the first and the whole third chapter of the *Systematic Theology* are devoted to it—but the more formidable foe is that of mysticism. The followers of Schleiermacher exhibited the tendency to erect the feelings of the individual above the objective facts and doctrines of the Christian faith. In Hodge's opinion this was a wholly misguided theological method. Perhaps it appeared so dangerous to Hodge because he was predisposed on occasions, according to the testimony of his intimate friends, to be overcome by his own emotions. This is evidenced also by his account of his very sensitive childhood religious experiences. While this may be true and should not be wholly discounted. Hodge's opposition probably stemmed most directly from what he considered to be the teaching of the Scriptures and the church.

McAllister has shown that Scottish philosophy also greatly influenced his thinking at this point. Hodge always insisted that his theology was not dependent upon philosophy but was simply the teaching of the Scriptures and the Reformed tradition extending back to Calvin. He simply asserted that without the objective facts of the Christian religion, Christian experience would not be possible. God's revelation in the Scriptures was primary. Without that revelation man would be ignorant of God's plan of salvation. However, since God has objectively revealed his plan of salvation and brought it to completion in Jesus Christ, man can be saved. What the believer experiences and feels is based on something objective. Hodge retained the necessity of the Holy Spirit's revealing the truth to the individual, but his emphasis on the ability of man to have some knowledge of God by the exercise of reason and the assumption that this knowledge is correct as far as it goes, introduces an implicit rationalism, which his mentor John Calvin would have sharply criticized. Perhaps the root of Hodge's departure from Calvin's thinking is in his attributing secondary importance to the witness of the Spirit in his chapter on methodology. The very fact that he states that "the inward teaching of the Spirit, or religious experience, is no substitute for an external revelation"[76] has the appearance of posing an "either . . . or" between the Scriptures and the work of the Spirit rather than seeing the two as co-witnesses. According to Calvin the Scriptures alone are insufficient without the inner witness of the Spirit in one's experi-

---

76. *ST*, I, p. 16.

ence, while on the other hand man's experience is judged by God's Word. The two function correlatively. To ask which is more important, which Hodge did on several occasions and always stated that there can be only one ultimate authority—the Scriptures—is to ask a misguided question. Calvin's theology was consistently a scriptural one, but it did not occur to him to separate these two witnesses from one another.

While these criticisms of Hodge's theology point out a certain dependence on reason and an intellectualistic cast to his thinking, the main object of this section of our investigation has been to point out the presence of subjective emphases in Hodge's formal writings. As in Alexander's thought, frequent appeal is made to the religious experience of believers. Hodge contends that one's theology is determined not only from the Scriptures but from one's experience when it has been authenticated by the Scriptures. Hymns, liturgies, and the devotional experiences of Christians in the church are products of the religious feelings. The specific doctrines of Christianity are of such a heavenly nature that intellectual assent alone is impossible as the only response. The believer's feelings are aroused, and he experiences such gifts as peace and joy. And from this experience arise numerous theologies of the feelings. So legitimate are these experiences that hymns or devotional diaries are valid expressions of them and the contents of Scripture.

Although Schleiermacher's theology, specifically, and subjective or mystical theology, in general, were the main foci of attack in the *Systematic Theology* and *The Way of Life,* the critique of excesses of revivalism did not cease with Princeton's first professor but was picked up and developed even more sharply by his successor in the second of his two-volume work on the history of the Presbyterian church. The volume covered the period 1741–1788. The first section of the book concerned the first Great Awakening. He admitted that the church was in need of revival in that period. In fact the decline of religion in America and in Great Britain was due not to the wide prevalence of false doctrine but to "a coldness and sluggishness with regard to religion." What was even more serious was that "in some cases the ministers, though orthodox, knew nothing of experimental religion."[77] Hodge, therefore, demanded the necessity of experimental religion and, like Alexander before him, recognized that revival is imperative when dead orthodoxy is the prevailing state of religion. Unless people are converted and

---

77. Hodge, *The Constitutional History of the Presbyterian Church in the United States of America,* 2: 16.

live holy lives, dead orthodoxy is as useless as speculative philosophy for it does not lay hold upon its object.

Hodge's assessment of the revival is similar to Alexander's. He uses the same criteria for evaluating the revival. The genuineness of a revival is easily ascertained by applying certain criteria to the movement in question. The first is that the doctrines preached are to be compared with the central doctrines of the Christian faith. If the doctrines do not accord with such doctrines as justification by faith, original sin, regeneration by the Holy Spirit, and repentance, then the proportionate purity of revival is reduced. The second criterion used to evaluate a revival is the kind of experience propagated. Hodge repeats Alexander's dictum that the experience of all true Christians is essentially the same, such as conviction of sin, desire for deliverance, and dependence on the work of Christ for salvation.

> These acts of faith will ever be attended with more or less of joy and peace, and with a desire and purpose to live in obedience to the will of God. The distinctness and strength of these exercises, the rapidity of their succession, their modifications and combinations, admit of endless diversity, yet they are all to be found in every case of genuine conversion.[78]

The third criterion is the effects of the revival on the lives of the people. Profession of revival should manifest itself over a period of time in the lives of the people who participated in it. Hodge cites Jonathan Edwards's testimony in the case of Northampton as an example. The fact that in that area where the revival had supposedly been most successful, the decline of religion that followed in its wake was the most pronounced "is certainly *prima facie* proof that there must have been something very wrong in the revival itself."[79]

What distinguishes Hodge's account of revival experience from Alexander's are the denunciations of various individuals by name for allowing the emotional excesses to take place and the rather lengthy detail into which Hodge goes to identify the emotional outbursts with mental disorders. These two are rather closely linked since his disparagement of certain men is based not only on their failure to take precautions against the expression of violent feelings but on what Hodge considered their tendency to judge their effectiveness on these outbursts. Hodge recognized that some expression of emotion is valid. He mentions a letter of Tennent written to a Rev. Prince in

---

78. Ibid., p. 50.
79. Ibid., p. 59.

Boston, which states that no enthusiasm was evident in one particular instance of his preaching. There were no visions "except such as are by faith; namely clear and affecting views of the new and living way to the Father through his dear Son Jesus Christ" and no revelations "but what have been long since written in the sacred volume."[80] He also cites a Samuel Blair in Pennsylvania who reported instances of crying, fainting, and "strange convulsive agitations of the body." What was worthy of approval, however, was that most who were thus affected "were influenced by a fixed and rational conviction of their dangerous condition." They not only agreed with the Bible as to its doctrines but also evidenced peace and joy and other fruits of the Holy Spirit as well.[81]

Hodge includes a lengthy analysis of the revival under Edwards at Northampton and sharply criticizes Edwards for allowing the emotional phenomena to continue under his ministry. He mentions reports of people lying in a trance who imagined that they went to heaven and had glorious visions. "When the people were raised to this height, Satan took the advantage, and his interpositions, in many instances, soon became apparent, and a great deal of pains was necessary to keep the people from running wild."[82] Hodge then argues that if such experiences occurred under Edwards, who was known for his judgment and piety, what could be expected from men who were inferior in judgment? Hodge is careful to mention that Edwards insisted that emotional phenomena did not guarantee the purity of the participants' religious affections. Nevertheless, he did not exercise proper caution in allowing the outbursts to continue.

> He was at this time much less sensible of the dangers of encouraging such manifestations of excitement, than he afterwards became. Nor does he seem to have been sufficiently aware of the nature and effects of nervous disorders, which in times of excitement are as infectious as any form of disease, to which the human system is liable. When he speaks of certain persons being seized with a strange bodily affection, which quickly propagated itself round the room . . . he gives as plain an example of the sympathetic propagation of a nervous disorder, as is to be found in the medical records of disease.[83]

Leaving aside momentarily the discussion of revivalistic behavior as examples of nervous disorders, it is obvious that Hodge has gone farther than

---

80. Ibid., pp. 22-23.
81. Ibid., p. 31.
82. Ibid., p. 41.
83. Ibid., pp. 41-42.

Alexander by criticizing people by name. Whitefield and Tennent receive equally sharp rebukes, Whitefield for his harsh judgment of other people's experience in comparison with his own and Tennent for judging the religious condition of other ministers. He also justly condemns the excesses of Davenport's ministry. But Hodge did not group men like Edwards and Davenport together indiscriminately. He was specific in his evaluation. In the opening pages of his section on revivalism he stated that some of the best and some of the worst men in the church were involved in the revival on both sides of the issue. Unfortunately two men of such contrasting spirits as Edwards and Davenport were both identified as supporters of the movement.[84]

Hodge launched a strident attack against what he considered to be the revival's emotional extremes. Too often genuine experiences of repentance due to divine influence were confused with mere wild outcries. In Whitefield's ministry, for example, both genuine and spurious experiences were manifest. Hodge attributed the spurious experiences to Whitefield's "vivid descriptions of hell, of heaven, of Christ, and a future judgment." He claimed that "striking appeals to the passions were delivered with consummate skill of voice and manner."[85] But since genuine experiences of repentance also resulted from such preaching, Hodge delineated what he considered to be the legitimate use of the imagination in religion.

The Scripture repeatedly presents pictures that appeal to the imagination when speaking of Christ, the church, and heaven. But the figure is always secondary to the reality signified. In true religious experience the mind apprehends the reality behind the figure and avoids being inflamed with "mere curious excitement."[86] In the revivals it would have been folly to ask people to discriminate between imaginary creations of the mind and legitimate spiritual apprehensions because pressure was constantly exerted upon people to experience mental images. The more intense and vivid, the more religious they were supposed to be.

> Under such instruction they would strive to form such imaginations; they would dote on them; inflame themselves with them and consider the vividness of the image, and the violence of the consequent emotion, as the measure of their religious attainment.[87]

---

84. Ibid., pp. 12, 83-90.
85. Ibid., p. 66.
86. Ibid., p. 68.
87. Ibid.

What confounded the situation was that such outbreaks of emotion affected the uneducated and those who had nervous temperaments more than the educated. These were more likely to succumb to the effects of mass sympathy. Hodge appealed to several medical authorities in support of his view. Such nervous disorders, according to Hodge, are likely to occur whenever conditions exist that encourage excitement. The occasion of their arising may differ greatly from the presence of fanaticism or superstition to the preaching of the truth from Scriptures. But if preaching encourages the abuse of the imagination, evidences of nervous disorders will inevitably result. While the impure is mixed with the pure, it is relatively easy to distinguish between the two when they become confused. The effects of genuine religious feeling are well known. They affect not the heated imagination, but the moral emotions and give rise to a change in one's behavior.

Finally Hodge asserts that these phenomena are unknown in the Bible. Bodily agitation, fainting, and crying did not accompany the preaching of either Christ or the apostles. He admits that such events as the Philippian jailor crying, "What must I do to be saved?" and Paul's dramatic conversion on the road to Damascus contain elements of strong emotion, but in the final analysis Hodge insists that such instances are not to be compared with the examples of hysterical behavior that are reported among the revivals. He is content to stand by the Presbyterian example, which could serve as a foundation for faithful preaching.

Alexander's hope had been that the necessity for periods of revival might be obviated in the future not because conversion would become unnecessary but because the preaching that people would hear and their education in the Scriptures would be such that conversions would be normal occurrences rather than the exceptions in the local church. Alexander's plan was not that people would be made better because they had been catechized by their parents thus substituting naturalistic improvement through education for genuine conversion. Instead miniature revivals would be occurring continuously within the local churches because people would be familiar with the Scripture, the plan of salvation, and the work of Christ and would readily respond either to teaching in the home or preaching in the pulpit. If such were the case periodic revivals, which always seem to bring with them great excitement in the form of emotional expression and subsequent religious decline, might be avoided.

Hodge simply expanded on Alexander's projected solution for the problem caused by periodic surges of revival. His views are most consistently set forth in his review of Horace Bushnell's *Discourses on Christian Nurture*. Despite what were considerable differences in the theologies of the two men, Hodge found much to advocate in Bushnell's views. His main objection to Bushnell's view of Christian nurture was its naturalistic cast: "The whole tenor of this book is in favour of the idea that all true religion is gradual, habitual, acquired as habits are formed. Everything must be like a natural process, nothing out of the regular sequence of cause and effect."[88] Despite this one glaring weakness which does not allow for the supernatural work of the Holy Spirit in regenerating the soul, Hodge found much that was commendable. He paid the book the highest accolade in saying that its general theme and specifically the phrase "Christian nurture" "has power to give his Discourses very much of an 'Old-school' cast, and to render them in a high degree attractive and hopeful in our estimation."[89] What made Bushnell's views attractive was his insistence that the revivals were stressed to the relative depreciation of the role of education in the home as a means of bringing up Christian children. Bushnell stressed the importance of the community and its common life rather than focusing only on the individual and his relation with God.

Hodge modified but did not substantially change Bushnell's main points. Hodge believed that the relation between the piety of parents and that of their children is a divinely constituted relation, which should lead parents to expect their children to become children of God. Bushnell attributes this to a natural process in which the "natural pravity may be overcome by Christian nurture, and a real regeneration effected by parental character" in a natural way.[90] Hodge's confidence in the relation between the parents' and the children's piety is based instead on the covenant promises and providence of God. Hodge gives a detailed analysis of the Abrahamic covenant and covenant theology in general to indicate that God has promised that if parents obey the covenant themselves and train their children in it, they can expect God to bless their efforts by bringing them to repentance and faith.

Parental training, therefore, can become the means for the salvation of their children. Hodge's description of Christian nurture is intended to

---

88. "Discourses on Christian Nurture," *Biblical Repertory and Princeton Review*, 19, no. 4 (1847): 533.

89. Ibid., p. 502. He also states "We anticipate immeasurably more good than evil from its publication" (p. 504). The reference to "Old-school" is a means of praising the work. The Princeton men consistently took the "Old-school" position on matters of doctrine and policy in disputes in the Presbyterian church between "Old-school" and "New-school" factions. Cf. Loetscher, op. cit., pp. 1-8, 21-28.

90. "Discourses on Christian Nurture," p. 536.

replace Bushnell's naturalism, and it clearly reflects his education by his mother.

> From its earliest infancy . . . the child is the object of tender solicitude, and the subject of many believing prayers. The spirit which reigns around it is the spirit, not of the world, but of true religion. . . . The child is sedulously guarded as far as possible from all corrupting influence, and subject to those which tend to lead him to God . . . The child thus trained grows up in the fear of God; his earliest experiences are more or less religious.[91]

Hodge assumed that with such a Christian atmosphere in the covenant family the child will be nurtured in the faith during childhood and eventually come to faith. Christian nurture should be the expected means by which people train their children with a view to mature Christian commitment in adulthood. This method, however, is not without its weaknesses. Christian nurture can easily degenerate into an empty formalism. The temptation for both parents and children to think that "religion consists entirely in knowledge and orthodoxy" is to be warded off by adherence to the Scriptures, believing in God's testimony contained therein and "at the same time looking constantly for the vivifying presence and power of his Spirit."[92] This leads Hodge yet another time to define Christianity "subjectively considered" as the supernatural work of God in man's soul.

> We are raised from spiritual death and so united to Christ as to become partakers of his life; and . . . this life is maintained and promoted, not by any mere rational process of moral culture, but by the constant indwelling of the Spirit of Christ. . . . Religion, therefore, or Christianity subjectively considered, is not something natural . . . it is . . . the life of God in the soul.[93]

By this description Hodge succeeds in ameliorating some of the rationalistic connotations found elsewhere in his definition of Christian faith. In this instance he takes pains not to identify faith wholly with the working of reason. The necessity of the Holy Spirit's working is also clearly emphasized. When the foe is Schleiermacher, the same definition of Christianity subjectively considered is appropriated as when the foe is a full-blown naturalism. When opposing Schleiermacher, Hodge emphasizes the work of the Spirit and the importance of knowledge. When facing Bushnell

---

91. Ibid., pp. 509-10.
92. Ibid., p. 515.
93. Ibid., p. 517.

the situation is reversed, and in this instance Hodge clearly discerns the dangers of rationalism and carefully avoids them.

Hodge is even more explicit in his view of teaching piety to children in his "Review of Sprague's Lectures to Young People."

> . . . the mode of exhibition must be adapted to the comprehension of the child. Nothing is gained where nothing is understood. The mere storing the memory with abstract propositions, although embodying the most truth, can have no effect on the present character of the child.[94]

The best method is to engender in the child a feeling of dependence on God: "That this God is good and merciful, the child may be made to feel."[95] Hodge's treatment of Christian nurture contains an explicit rebuke of those who have come to view revivalism as the only means to convert people to Christ. Christians who are convinced of the supernatural character of Christianity and yet have depended on revivals rather than Christian nurture for the conversion of their children have not only misplaced their confidence but have manifested a distorted view of the Christian family life. They assume that their children will grow up living lives of sin until under the influences of a revival they make a dramatic change of behavior following a sudden experience. Such a view ignores God's design of the covenant family relationship. God's grace can be manifest in a gradual as well as in a sudden change of life.

From a biographical standpoint Hodge's argument reveals the reason for his high regard of his mother and the religious training he had in his youth. The memories of his childhood religious experience seem to stand out in greater relief than his own conversion experience while he was as Princeton. Of the latter we know almost nothing, while he speaks of the former with great feeling. The indication given in the first section of this chapter regarding Hodge's family life and the great affection expressed between him and his children is also further illuminated by this discussion of Christian nurture. In both cases several factors, including catechizing and inculcating knowledge by memorizing the Scriptures and prayers, created what Hodge advocated—a believing and trusting atmosphere which was best described not in terms of the information conveyed but in terms of the feeling engendered. Hodge and his children describe their family relationship in words of endearment. They expressed their feelings of love toward one another and

---

94. *Biblical Repertory and Theological Review*, 3, no. 3 (1831): 300.
95. Ibid.

toward God in a very childlike way. Childlike expressions of affection were not childish phenomena to be superseded later by intellectual knowledge. Intellectual knowledge might at times assume a more prominent position, as has been noted in our examination of the *Systematic Theology,* but Hodge's conception of Christian knowledge contains this experiential element, which is illuminated by this discussion of Christian nurture and reflected in his piety and his children's.

Summary of Hodge's Formal Writings

Charles Hodge carried forward the tradition begun by Archibald Alexander by continuing to wage an essentially two-front attack against rationalists and speculative philosophers on the one hand and the "mystics" and revivalists on the other. While the emphasis has changed somewhat, the essential patterns are the same. What has changed is the result of the appearance of a more formidable foe in Schleiermacher's theology. Both Hodge and Alexander take the same position against revivalists although Hodge's opposition is stronger. A more pronounced dependence on the Scottish philosophy and Turretine's theology is also found in Hodge's writings. This was undoubtedly due in part to the nature of Hodge's writings, for Alexander never wrote a systematic theology. Nevertheless, the number of references to these men, especially Turretine, in the *Systematic Theology,* indicates the dependence that he made on them.[96] But his opposition to subjectivism led him to draw a sharper line between the Scriptures and the witness of the Spirit. The witness of the Spirit is far from denied, but it is clearly subordinate to the Word. But this subordination did not prevent Hodge from appealing to the experience of believers and emphasizing that the best source for finding out what Christians believe is the record of their hymns, liturgies, and devotional writings.

Hodge consistently retained the importance of internal evidence, but the strongest argument for it appeared in *The Way of Life* and not in his *magnum opus.* In this more popular exposition of his theology the experiential element is permitted to dominate his discussion. It may be possible that the *Systematic Theology* represents Hodge's theology of the intellect and that Hodge himself intended *The Way of Life* to represent his theology of the feelings. If so, it is clear that they meet the most important requirement set

---

96. The index of the *ST* includes 17 references to Turretine as compared to over 20 to Calvin and almost 30 to Augustine.

forth in his discussion with Park, that they are identical in nature and can in no way contradict one another.

In making explicit what was implicit in Alexander's theology regarding the subjective and objective definitions of Christianity, Hodge has retained the emphasis initiated by his predecessor. Objectively considered, Christianity consists of certain historical and scriptural facts which form the basis of doctrinal and creedal statements. The term "Christianity" has objective content to which assent can be given. However, and not just as an addendum but as a way of completing our understanding of the term, "Christianity" has a subjective aspect as well, which renders assent useless unless it is included. Faith without feelings is as empty and ineffectual as it is without assent. While some may argue that Hodge's definition of faith is much too intellectual and scholastic, the element of feeling on which Hodge continually insists is not an empty echo following the loud defense of intellectual assent but is in reality the crowning element that makes faith complete and sets it in opposition to the speculative opinions of philosophers. Just as faith without assent is merely a product of the individual's imagination, so faith without feelings is dead orthodoxy.

This does not eliminate other strongly intellectualistic elements of Hodge's theology, some of which this study has pointed out and others that should be mentioned, lest the idea be given that they are not present. Already mentioned are Hodge's conception of theology as a science and his rigid adherence to scientific method in doing theological formulations, which often results in merely using a prooftext approach. Chapter 3 in his *Systematic Theology,* while containing a refutation of the rationalists, also has a section on the proper office of reason in religion, which includes such elements as judging the credibility of a revelation.[97] Hodge also includes a lengthy discussion of the traditional arguments for the existence of God.[98] The inclusion of such material in his theology is directly in opposition to the thought of Calvin, whose theology he attempted to defend, and is an implicit acceptance of the capacities of human reason.

Despite the presence of such elements in his thinking, the experiential elements are far from lacking. The experience Hodge describes most is that of the believer subsequent to regeneration. The Christian life is dynamic and manifests such experiences as peace and joy and faith, which work by love.

97. *ST,* I, pp. 49-55. Hodge is most concerned to emphasize that man is not called upon to believe what is impossible. Christian faith is not irrational. Faith is based on adequate evidence both internal and external.
98. Ibid., pp. 204-40.

Hodge defined the religious life in terms that find their counterpart in the private devotional life of the believer. The Spirit illuminates the Scriptures so that the believer experiences different aspects of the text he had never seen before. His conception of sanctification involves the believer's partaking of the Spirit and thus being united with Christ. However, in the writings examined thus far the main knowledge that the Christian has is knowledge about Christ mediated by the Spirit through the Scriptures. This is the knowledge by contemplation that was noticed in Alexander's thought. There are glimpses of knowledge by communion, but these are the exception rather than the rule. The contrast between Hodge's own Christian experience, which was discussed in the first section of this chapter, and the formal description, which has been examined in this section, has been summed up very well by John O. Nelson:

> in dealing with the central and ultimate Christian teaching of redemption of the believer by Christ—which Hodge profoundly, daily experienced himself—the warmth of his conviction contrasts strangely with the legalism by which he supports it. [99]

Hodge's Devotional Writings

It was noted in the opening pages of this study that Hodge left his impress upon his students not primarily through his systematic writings and his lectures in the classroom, but through his own personal piety and his messages in the Sunday afternoon conferences in the oratory. Hodge himself testified to the problems that ensued from his teaching in the classroom. The format he used was essentially the same method Alexander used: assigning questions using Turretine as a text. But it soon became evident that students became adept in the skills of stenography. His lectures were copied and passed down from one student generation to another, so that they had copies not only of the questions and the answers, but also well-formulated theologies that had already been constructed by former students. This procedure, according to Hodge's son, became bothersome to both Hodge and his students since they had before them what was being read by the professor. This tedium was apparently overcome to a considerable extent after Hodge had published his theology. He felt liberated to a great degree from his former method and used in its place a system of spontaneous

99. John O. Nelson, "Charles Hodge, Nestor of Orthodoxy," *The Lives of Eighteen from Princeton*, ed. Willard Thorp, p. 209.

questioning which required students to gather their thoughts and give original expression to their views.[100]

But it was Hodge's gift of preaching that had a greater impact on his students. He preached not only in the seminary but also in the village church and throughout the neighboring towns. His preaching in the earlier part of his career was "more fresh and animated" than during his later years, according to his son.[101] The greatest praise was given to his efforts in the Sunday afternoon conferences. The format of the meeting was unchanged. A volume was published containing many of these short addresses. Many of them are mere outlines of what Hodge planned to say spontaneously during the meeting. Others are cogent, carefully worded statements.

The most significant sermons for the purpose of this study are those dealing with the nature of the contemplative and communal experience. Hodge frequently preached on subjects that led him to consider contemplation or meditation, and the general principle advocated was in keeping with the maxim of the primary importance of internal evidence. Since the Scriptures bear the impress of the Creator, when the believer reads the Scriptures it is not a mere reading of moral or religious statements but a spiritual experience by which one perceives the divine perfection revealed. The mind is engaged; the will is stimulated; and the heart is moved.

When Hodge exhorts his hearers to read the Scriptures, it is never merely to accumulate intellectual knowledge. Sometimes the exhortation is for Christians to consider certain important topics or responsibilities to stimulate a specific action. It was thus, in a missionary conference address on Matthew 9:37: "The harvest truly is plenteous, but the laborers are few," and the duty of Christians is to "let this subject . . . come before you in all its solemn importance, and let it weigh constantly on your minds."[102] But besides allowing specific subjects and texts to make their impressions, which was implicit in all the sermons of the Princeton men, one of the most important of Christian duties was to meditate on the Scriptures as a normal part of the believer's spiritual life. In a conference sermon on the subject "Meditation as a Means of Grace" Hodge pointed out the main distinction between meditation and mere intellectual consideration of an idea. The object of the latter is merely to understand intellectually while the object of meditation is to experience the power of God's Word. He outlines specific

100. *LCH*, pp. 323-24, 387-88.
101. Ibid., p. 205.
102. Ibid., p. 329.

suggestions to aid in this exercise. Believers ought to purpose to do this faithfully, setting aside times when it might be regularly performed. It should be done concomitantly with prayer, i.e., "not only in the formal sense of the word, but also as meaning converse with God."[103] In another sermon on "Prayer" Hodge encourages his hearers to store "the mind with Scriptural expressions" as a preparation for prayer since these expressions are those forms in which "the Holy Ghost has given utterance to the thoughts and feelings which we desire to express."[104]

In still other sermons dealing with meditation more practical suggestions are made. Drawing on the analogy of appreciating beauty in nature by means of prolonged aesthetic appreciation, Hodge states that the believer may use the Scriptures in a similar manner in meditation.

> The great doctrines of the Scriptures must in like manner be contemplated with a steady and protracted gaze, and here too, as in the analogous cases, it is passivity that is required. It is not active discriminating thought, but clear and constant vision that is necessary. The same remark is applicable to particular passages of Scripture. . . . If God should give us grace, we might sit down before it and gaze on its ever expanding wonders and glories until *we were transformed and translated*. Such is not now our duty.[105]

Although the full impact of this particular passage is slightly lessened by the concluding sentence, what precedes can hardly be overemphasized. The suggestion of mystical experience is undeniably present. This, of course, may have occasioned Hodge to add the concluding sentence lest the impression be given that the Princeton Calvinist advocates mystical retreat from the world. But the advocacy of a "steady and protracted gaze" leading to being "transformed and translated" is indeed unexpected language. Contemplation as a spiritual experience was no casual intellectual exercise. Hodge intimates that were this now our duty experiences analogous to those of heavenly existence would result.

Hodge also elaborated on the greatest obstacle that stands in one's way of enjoying the blessings derived from it; the absence of Christ—the object of our love—from our presence.

> Dear Brethren . . . He is absent. A thousand other objects . . . intervene and thrust him from our minds. Alas—he is seldom present to

---

103. Ibid., p. 299.
104. Ibid., p. 294.
105. Ibid., p. 244 (emphasis mine).

our thoughts at all . . . and how often by some slight association does the world entice the mind away and Jesus is forgotten. How indistinct and vague too are all our conceptions of his glory. . . . We have, therefore, much to hope from the taring [sic] aside the veil. When once we see him and are with him . . . Oh then our full hearts will swell with emotion.[106]

The strong emotional feeling that might be called upon in Hodge by the mere mention of Christ's death was to be cherished and cultivated.

One further instance in which Hodge enlarges his view of contemplation is especially significant. On several occasions Hodge encouraged believers to store up Scriptures in their minds to use in prayer and meditation. Hodge's sermons reflect this practice as did Alexander's. But Hodge's quotation of the Bible differs slightly from his predecessor's. It appears as if he has copied snatches of passages and strung them together. We might think that Hodge wrote with a concordance at his elbow. However, just enough words in these passages do not quite fit the Scriptures verbatim to indicate that Hodge in fact has called upon his familiarity with the Bible and has recalled these quotations from memory. The following is an example. I have inserted the reference from which the words or phrases probably originated. The theme of the sermon is the fatherly nature of God.

God did not give us up (Rom. 1:24). Having given us his Son he has with him freely given all things (Rom 8:32). He had sent his Holy Spirit to enlighten our minds (Eph. 1:18), to convince us of sin and misery (John 16:8), to renew our hearts (Psa. 51:10), to persuade and enable to embrace Jesus Christ as freely offered to us in the gospel (Eph. 1:6). He causes the Spirit to dwell within us (John 14:17), to lead us into the knowledge and obedience of the truth (John 16:13), to console us, to aid our infirmities (Rom. 8:26), to shed abroad his love in our hearts (Rom. 5:5)—and to bear witness with our spirits that we are the children of God.[107]

In such a passage, we find Hodge's pietistic or devotional love of the Scriptures, which all of the Princeton men exhibited. His defense of biblical authenticity and inspiration was only one evidence of a life that was devoted to upholding the word of truth. But such defense was anything but a mere intellectual exercise. The Scriptures were as much stored in his heart as in his mind.

106. "Unnumbered Sermons, Preached and Repreached between 1823-1876," "I Peter 1:8."
107. "Sermons, New Series 1-47, Preached and Repreached between 1842-1876," no. 5, "I John 5:5"

The fundamental question in evaluating Hodge's sermons is whether he in fact makes the transition from contemplation of the facts *of* Scripture or the doctrines *about* Christ to communion of the most personal nature between the individual and Christ. In the final analysis, is the deepest or most significant experiential level that of perceiving, knowing, and feeling the affections moved by doctrines about Christ, or knowing Christ in personal experience? McAllister in his thesis states: "for Hodge the trust element in faith has as its primary object not Christ the second Person of the Trinity, but doctrines about Christ which Hodge understood to be revealed in Scriptures."[108] McAllister claims that the propositional knowledge which is foremost in Hodge's theology lacks the qualities of interpersonal relationship that are found, for instance, in the writings of Paul and St. Augustine.

This is a crucial question if we are to maintain Hodge's balance on the objective-subjective issue. The propositional element plays a significant role in Hodge's thinking. It is the underlying assumption in his description of faith as assent, knowledge, and trust. We have seen that Hodge, considering his presuppositions, had significant justification for emphasizing the objective in Christianity to counter the growing dominance of subjectivism in theology. Hodge stressed the importance of an objective content to faith as a basis for confidence in and reliance upon the Scriptures. But it has also become clear that the Word also functions as a means by which one experientially knows the great truths of Christianity. Hodge was not a pure scholastic demanding a strictly rational assent to doctrinal propositions. Faith in Jesus Christ includes acceptance of what the Scriptures declare Him to be, i.e., Savior, Son of God, prophet, priest, and king. It also includes trust in these facts, i.e., that the promises associated with the facts and doctrines of Christianity are promises of a personal God. God will honor his promises to justify by His grace those who place their confidence in Him. Faith in God and in Christ is confidence that what God has revealed in His Word is true and that He will be true to what He has revealed.

But Hodge goes further than this and includes the element of personal communion between the believer and God or Christ. This element is based on the contemplative or meditative strand in his sermons. Communion with God goes beyond contemplation of God. Hodge explains in several of his sermons the added dimension that personal communion adds to spiritual experience. Communion is based first on the personal nature of God. In his

---

108. McAllister, op. cit., p. 272.

Systematic Theology Hodge emphasized that the doctrine of the Trinity includes the idea that Father, Son, and Spirit are persons.

> The Father, Son, and Spirit are severally subject and object. They act and are acted upon, or are the objects of action. Nothing is added to these facts when it is said that the Father, Son, and Spirit are distinct persons; for a person is an intelligent subject who can say I, who can be addressed as Thou, and who can act and can be the object of action.[109]

The personality of the Godhead is stressed even further when Hodge, in discussing the Holy Spirit, contends that the Spirit is not a mere power but a person with whom Christians sustain the same relation as they do with the Father and Son.

> We pray to the Spirit for the communication of Himself to us, that He may, according to the promise of our Lord, dwell in us, as we pray to Christ that we may be the objects of his unmerited love. . . . He is represented . . . as a person . . . whom we may please or offend; with whom we may have communion, i.e., personal intercourse; who can love and be loved; who can say "thou" to us; and whom we can involve in every time of need.[110]

The Spirit as personal has the greatest implication for one's definition of Christianity: "Christianity (subjectively considered) would not be what it is without this sense of dependence on the Spirit, and this love and reverence for his person. All the liturgies, prayers, and praises of the Church are filled with appeals and addresses to the Holy Ghost."[111]

In his sermons Hodge presents this doctrine of the personality of God as something which is to be contemplated so that it can have its full effect upon the feelings. In "The Love of Christ Constraineth Us" Hodge notes that Christ's love is not general benevolence but "the love of a particular person to a particular person." He notes the saying of the apostle Paul that God "loved *me*." This love is "tender, considerate, sympathizing." Hodge's exhortation then is for the hearers to let this fact be impressed upon them so that they will "feel the effect of the love of Christ dying for us."[112] But this idea of the personality of God also gave rise to several sermons on such subjects as "Friends of Jesus" and "Walking with God." In these messages Hodge states that our relation with God is similar to our relation with

---

109. *ST,* I, p. 444.
110. Ibid., p. 525.
111. Ibid., p. 526.
112. *Conference Papers,* p. 220; cf. pp. 199-200.

personal friends. A friend is one with whom we commune and to whom we can open our hearts. But our friends also commune with us. Our friendship with Christ is of a similar nature. Not only do we communicate our feelings to Christ but he communicates to us by the Scripture and the Spirit.[113] It is by the Scripture that we might expect Hodge to claim that Christ communicates to the believer. The presence of the Spirit needs further clarification. This is provided in the conference address "Walking with God." This experience is rare, in Hodge's opinion. More than casual intercourse with God is implied. We are continually aware of his presence and of our thoughts rising to him. But we also expect a response.

> Communion cannot be onesided. There must be conversation, address and answer. God does thus commune with us. He reveals himself to his people as he does not unto the world. He assures them of his love, He awakens in them confidence in his promises. He brings those promises to their minds, and gives them the power of response. These promises become his answers to their requests and they experience a renewal of faith, love, zeal, etc. . . . This is not imaginary. It is real. It is not enthusiasm. It does not suppose anything miraculous, no responses by voice, no unintelligent impulses; but the consciousness of the presence of the Infinite Spirit with our spirits; the conviction that he hears and answers us.[114]

It is clear that Hodge's priorities lie with the Spirit's use of the Word in man's communion with God. But Hodge's presuppositions, as in the case of Alexander, allowed him little leeway in this matter. To go beyond the work of the Spirit's using the Word bordered on revelation or inspiration, which had ceased with the Scriptures. Nevertheless, we are not left with knowledge merely *about* God and Christ. There is real truth in the knowledge the Spirit communicates by the Word.

Experience of communion with God is based on the nature of the union of the believer and Christ. Hodge was adamant that this union is not analogous to the mystical doctrine "of the absorption of the soul in God."[115] But it is more than something simply formal. The lowest interpretation that can be given of the nature of this union is that it is merely a union of sentiment and feeling. The union is capable of a more meaningful definition.

> Those who are Christ's are partakers of his life. It is not a mere external or federal union, nor a union of sentiment and feeling, but such a union

---

113. "Sermons," "John 5:15" (May 6, 1855).

114. *Conference Papers*, p. 254; cf. pp. 154-55.

115. Ibid., p. 26.

as exists between the branches and the vine, the members and the head of the body.

> It is only saying the same thing in other words to say that the Holy Ghost is given to all who are in Christ, to effect . . . deliverance from the power of sin. The Spirit descends from Christ to us, and Christ dwells in us by the Spirit.[116]

In another address the nature of the union is described as ''simply receiving Christ, becoming united to him, embracing him.''[117]

The depth of the experience to which this can lead is evident from some of the sermons containing language similar to that quoted from Alexander's sermons. In preaching on prayer as a means of grace Hodge stated that converse with God can be solemn and formal ''in the use of articulate words and on set occasions in the closet, family or sanctuary''; or it can be ejaculatory ''and thus constant, as the bubbling of a spring of living water''; or it can be on the highest level ''the unuttered aspirations and longings of the soul after God, like the constant ascent of the flame towards heaven.''[118] To the believer Christ is everywhere, and contemplation of him leads to experiences that are virtually impossible to describe.

> The more the soul contemplates his excellence the more does it gather of his brightness and when lost in the discoveries of the grandeurs of his deity . . . [it] sinks into nothing before the blaze of his glory. The thought that he 'loved me and gave himself for me' gives rise to feelings which know no utterance.[119]

> Do this, and see if the conviction does not overwhelm you with wonder and humility. See if you do not desire to be lost in the effulgence of the divine glory, so that he only may be praised.[120]

> The glory of God in the face of Jesus Christ is made so clear that we are ravished by it, delivered thereby from the love of sin and of the world.[121]

Just as in Alexander's sermons one cannot but acknowledge that although the emphasis is on communion with God through the Scriptures, yet the result of the concept of union with Christ through the Holy Spirit and

---

116. Ibid., p. 150; cf. pp. 150-51.

117. Ibid., p. 144.

118. Ibid., p. 291.

119. ''Unnumbered Sermons, Preached and Repreached between 1823-1876,'' ''I Peter 2:7.''

120. ''Sermons Preached and Repreached between 1825-1874,'' ''Eph. 1.19.''

121. Conference Papers, p. 197.

participation in Christ's life by this indwelling heightens the experience. The possibility of broaching absorption into the divine being never enters into consideration although Hodge poses the possibility of being "lost in the effulgence of the divine glory" and "ravished" by it. There is an ineffableness of experience that is vividly communicated, and mystical vocabulary characterizes these excerpts. It is almost as if Hodge had penned these words directly from his own feelings.

Having seen the wide diversity of Hodge's and Alexander's writings on religious experience one question remains to be discussed, and that concerns what might be regarded as the hiatus that exists in general between the systematic and devotional writings of these two men. This disparity, as a result of the discussion in this study, is not quite as great as might formerly have been supposed. Nevertheless, one is cognizant of a difference between the formal or didactic way in which theological issues are discussed in the systematic works and some of the passages from the devotional writings, which suggest a comparatively greater dependence on the emotive faculty. Undoubtedly a large part of this contrast can be explained by the significant difference in purpose between delivering lectures on didactic and polemic theology with an emphasis on conveying intellectual truth and preaching, which includes the elements of exhortation and persuasion as well as communication of knowledge. Perhaps, however, this discrepancy would never have occurred to these Princeton men. Not that they did not distinguish between the classroom and the oratory. But they saw both as part of a larger context. Truth, whether it be aesthetic or intellectual can be subsumed under the category of beauty. Beauty characterizes all that God has made or revealed whether it be the natural bridge in Virginia or the majestic Alps of Switzerland, or the beauty of a carefully reasoned and explicated theology, or the beauty of a soul regenerated and enthralled by the glory of God.

This is not to claim that Alexander and Hodge were mere romantics possessing a romantic vision of the world. But it is to say that their vision took in far more than internal and external evidences, the arguments for the existence of God, and the distinctions between speculative and saving faith. Their theological vision was based on the assumption that evidences of God's work are to be found in every area of life—from the natural world to the realms of intellectual, moral, and spiritual experience. Several examples of the Platonic mode of thought are to be found in Alexander's thinking. That which is most evident is his obvious appreciation for the beauties of nature. It was one of his fondest memories of his childhood that Rockbridge,

Virginia, besides having the natural bridge, which made a strong impression
on him in his youth, also had two other magnificent formations: House
Mountain and Jump Mountain. Alexander reminisced in his old age that it
was his lot "to draw the first breath of life at the foot of a lofty mountain, and
on the bank of a roaring mountain torrent; where the reveillé was often the
hideous howling of hungry wolves."[122]

A further example of Alexander's use of the concept of beauty was an
example he used to illustrate the difference that revelation makes between
speculative faith and saving faith. It bears a striking resemblance to Plato's
"Allegory of the Cave" from the *Republic*.

> A number of persons brought up in a cave, into which the rays of the sun
> never entered, if brought out, when this luminary was shining in its
> brightness, would need no arguments to prove its existence; they would
> have the evidence in themselves, in the shining of the light into their
> eyes, or, if placed where they could not see the sun, yet, where there
> was a reflection of his rays, they would need no further evidence of its
> existence.[123]

The new views one has are the result of revelation of God's Spirit. The
blindness of the human heart, more specifically the "blindness of nature,"
is removed and the light of "the glorious gospel will shine into such a
regenerated mind, revealing to it the beauty of holiness . . ." with the
result that "Christ appears lovely . . . and he becomes the jewel of their
hearts."[124] Platonic motifs are thus present in Alexander's thought. Grada-
tion and contemplation of various types of beauty are evident. The mind is
renewed, and while the objects of nature participate in beauty they are not to
be compared to the ultimate beauty of God's holiness as manifest in Christ.
The Christian perceives this beauty of holiness by means of contemplation
and the illumination of the mind by the Holy Spirit.

It remained for Hodge to elaborate a more detailed concept of beauty.
Whereas Alexander had explicitly mentioned only the objects of nature and
objects in the spiritual realm, Hodge added the intellectual and moral realms
as well, which provide the intermediate stages in the ascending ladder
between the physical order of creation and the spiritual realm. The first
reference that Hodge makes to beauty is an indirect one since it is in the form
of a quote from Joseph Bellamy, the disciple of Jonathan Edwards.

---

122. *LAA*, p. 25.
123. *Practical Sermons*, pp. 12, 13.
124. Ibid., p. 13. Cf. quotes on pp. 47, 73, 84, 97, 99 in the chapter on Alexander above.

In regeneration, there is a new, divine and holy task begotten in the heart, by the immediate influences of the Holy Spirit. . . . The idea of a natural beauty supposes an internal sense, implanted by our Creator, by which the mind is capacitated to discern such kind of beauty.[125]

Hodge's conception of this beauty is fully elaborated, however, in a conference sermon "Beauty of Holiness." He notes that although theories of τὸ κάλον have existed for centuries, the real meaning of beauty escapes complete definition. Beauty awakens a certain pleasure in the mind which is not sensual or moral but aesthetical. "This pleasure is a complacent delight in the object itself apart from its relation to us."[126]

Hodge enumerates the many different kinds of beauty from that of natural objects and works of art, to that of "the human countenance," and the beauty of "that woman a sister or mother, [which] excites a pleasure altogether peculiar to itself." But there is also an intellectual beauty.

There is a beauty which addresses itself to the understanding. That is, the objects of the intellect when perceived, excite a pleasure analogous to that produced by a beautiful sensible object; e.g., beauty of style, which is not mere rhythm, but fitness, perspicuity, attributes which address themselves to the intelligence. So there is a beauty in a demonstration, in a logical argument; there is the eloquence of logic.[127]

Hodge mentions moral beauty as well. But the highest beauty does not address itself to the eye, ear, intellect, or moral nature but to the spiritual life implanted in believers by regeneration. This is the beauty of holiness. Among its attributes are purity, opposition to evil, and "all positive moral excellence." What characterizes its perception by a person is not merely his approval, respect, fear, or reverence but "complacent delight." "It gives a peculiar pleasure, and that of the highest kind. . . . This beauty is revealed most clearly in the Lord Jesus Christ. He is represented as most beautiful. . . . The Church is represented as ravished with his beauty."[128] The beauty of holiness is identified with the work of the Holy Spirit in the life of the believer: "The beauty of holiness in us is the manifestation of God in us. The Spirit of God in us is the Spirit of glory."[129]

---

125. "Regeneration," *Biblical Repertory and Theological Review*, 2, no. 2, (1830): 269-70.
126. *Conference Papers*, p. 211.
127. Ibid. p. 212.
128. Ibid.
129. Ibid.

The final instance in which Hodge alluded to this concept of beauty is in a lecture delivered in the seminary upon his arrival home from his studies in Europe in 1828. Part of the message deals with the subject of religious affections, and he makes a direct connection between piety and doctrine. But he also touches on the subject of beauty by drawing an analogy between what destroys an observer's aesthetic appreciation of natural beauty and what destroys a believer's feelings toward theological truth. Drawing undoubtedly from his own awe-struck experience at the foot of the Alps, he supposes a person who is overcome by the grandeur and beauty of an Alpine scene. However, he asks rhetorically, what happens when the same man rather than contemplating the beauty in aesthetic appreciation begins instead to consider geological structure of the rock formations? By simply analyzing rock structure and the geological aspects of the mountains the sense of beauty is lost. The grandeur is gone.[130]

The analogy can be drawn between this experience and a Christian's appreciation of religious truth. The contemplation and appreciation of theological truth as the reflection of divine revelation gives rise to devotion and the deepest of the religious affections. But when such truth is merely analyzed and metaphysically examined, this appreciation of the affections is destroyed as well. He asks, "Where is our reverence and awe of God, when prying into his essence or scrutinizing his attributes? Where is our feeling of penitence, when disputing on the origin of evil? our sense of responsibility when discussing free will and dependence?"[131] From the rest of Hodge's theology it is clear that these subjects must be broached, but never at the expense of losing one's religious affections and an appreciation of the beauty of holiness which such truths reflect. While Hodge does not explicitly draw this connection in this passage, it is certainly implied by the analogy that he draws from aesthetic appreciation of nature. People can be blind to an appreciation for the beauty of holiness manifested in doctrinal truths by simply taking into consideration only the metaphysical aspects of the statements just as they can miss the beauty of a scene by seeing only the scientific structure of its constituent objects.

At least one of Hodge's intimate friends alluded to this appreciation of

---

130. C. S. Lewis's argument for retaining a sense of objective value or wonder as a part of a Christian view of science is strikingly similar to Hodge's argument. Cf. *The Abolition of Man*, (New York).

131. "Lecture Addressed to the Students of the Theological Seminary, Nov. 7, 1828," p. 96.

beauty on the part of the Princeton professor. The commemorative discourse of Lyman H. Atwater delivered at Hodge's funeral is typical of the tributes paid to Hodge. While praising him for his "intensely logical" mind Atwater also called attention to the emotional characteristics of his personality. He cautions against any conclusion that this theologian was simply a "dry reasoner . . . without any imagination." Apart from an imaginative faculty such as Hodge possessed, "which 'mediates truth to the mind through beauty,' no man, however mighty as a reasoner, can put his reasonings in such a costume as to sway the minds of his fellowmen."[132] Whether we consider the intellectual presentation of the Christian faith or the intensely emotional nature of his personal piety, we notice his preoccupation with various manifestations of beauty.

Thus, for Alexander and Hodge everything that God has made reflects beauty. The world lies under sin, but it is a world that still reflects the beauty residing in the being of God. We perceive the impress of the divine perfection in the works of nature, in the Scriptures, in doctrine, in the fine points of a theological discourse, in a carefully exposited sermon, in the religious affections, and ultimately in the holiness of Jesus Christ. Beauty is perceived not only because God is its Creator but because he has also opened the eyes of the believer to see it. While the Princeton men admitted that a kind of graded scale exists from the works of nature to the beauty of holiness, they do not advocate starting with the natural and ascending by contemplation to a pure abstract and impersonal "form" of beauty. Only the person illuminated by the Holy Spirit perceives the whole scale of beauty and it culminates not with a depreciation of natural beauty and a rational perception of an abstract essence; the Christian has a view that encompasses all of reality and culminates in communion with the God of holiness who ravishes the believer with his glory as a foretaste of the heavenly beatific vision.

Just as no hiatus exists between the created order and the eternal order, insofar as both are attributed to God, Hodge and Alexander would have denied any essential disparity between their theologies and their devotional lives. They would have denied it not only because provision for the religious affections is made in their systematic writings, but ultimately because both their theologies and their devotional lives, their heads and their hearts, were really united. This was betrayed at times, i.e., when it was assumed that the oratory was for practical matters and the classroom for systematic theology. However, it has been evident from the sermons we have examined from both

132. Atwater, op. cit., p. 17.

men that some sermons are simply the explication of Scripture with exhortations added and that portions of their systematic works were much with the religious affections. Beauty is exhibited to both the head and the heart. Neither is complete without the other. The believer attributes the perception of both to the indwelling Holy Spirit.

CHAPTER THREE

BENJAMIN B. WARFIELD: PRINCETON APOLOGIST

The Princeton line of succession from Alexander to Hodge to Warfield is a broken one. Following Charles Hodge in the chair of systematic theology at Princeton was his son, Archibald Alexander Hodge. A. A. Hodge's role in the formation of the Princeton theology is relatively small due to his short tenure as professor from 1877-1887. He did not publish widely as did the other three men, but he did publish *Outlines of Theology* (1860), which received much acclaim from adherents of the Princeton viewpoint.[1] Therefore, our attention is turned to his successor, Benjamin B. Warfield.

Warfield is most famous as the great apologist of Princeton theology. He developed his apologetic not in a *magnum opus* but in a series of articles published in journals, dictionaries, and encyclopedias. Francis L. Patton mentions several reasons why he did not write his own theology. His devotion to teaching in the seminary, his involvement in controversy with viewpoints opposing the Princeton position, and his own bent for dealing primarily with doctrinal issues individually and not systematically all contributed to his failure to publish a systematic theology. But undoubtedly the greatest deterrent was his respect for and dependence on his teacher's *Systematic Theology,* as Patton intimates in his reference to Warfield's use of Hodge's work: "Dr. Warfield was not the man to turn the key of that temple and leave it to the moles and to the bats."[2]

An overwhelming continuity exists in the succession from Alexander through Hodge to Warfield. But a certain discontinuity exists as well due to the differing historical and theological contexts each man faced. Alexander's position on religious experience was determined almost wholly by his resolution to forge a *via media* between two factions in the Presbyterian church. In Hodge we noted that theologies from Europe attracted his attention, and, while Princeton's interest in revivalism did not cease, the focal

---

1. Cf. C. A. Salmond, ed., *Princetonia: Charles and A. A. Hodge: with Class and Table Talk of Hodge the Younger.* Also Loetscher, op. cit., pp. 30-32 for the collaboration between the younger Hodge and Warfield in the article "Inspiration" which appeared in the *Presbyterian Review,* 1881.
2. "Benjamin B. Warfield, A Memorial Address," *Princeton Theological Review,* 19 (1921): 387.

95

point of the Princeton theology became its opposition to the rise of modern theology. As the nineteenth century progressed, however, still additional trends clashing with the Princeton position loomed on the horizon. Although revivalism was far from spent, Warfield wrote more extensively on what he considered to be another outgrowth of the New Divinity theology adopted by the Oberlin School—perfectionism. Other more formidable threats appeared, which while known to his predecessors had not assumed the prominence they enjoyed when Warfield assumed the chair of theology at Princeton at the end of the nineteenth century. William D. Livingstone in his study of the Princeton apologetic lists those items against which Warfield waged his attack: the theologies of Schleiermacher and Ritschl from abroad and Taylor and Bushnell in America, biblical criticism as exemplified in the Tubingen School, evolutionary science, and the revival of Kantian philosophy.[3] While Alexander and Hodge fought several of these issues, by the time Warfield became professor of theology not only had the number of opposing viewpoints grown, but their wider acceptance among theologians in America was rapidly becoming a *fait accompli*. Just as his predecessors had not failed to confront any challenge to their Presbyterian orthodoxy, Warfield did not hesitate to take up the gauntlet thrown down by the allied forces of theology, science, and philosophy. His weapon was to be apologetics. Livingstone points out that in light of the attack being made on what Warfield considered the Christian position, apologetics took on a new and comprehensive element. Not only was the science of apologetics to defend or vindicate Christianity, but it was to *establish* Christianity firmly as the one absolute system of truth for all men. The purpose of apologetics in the past was to defend Christianity against charges made against it. But this defensive posture was to be allied with a full scale attack. Warfield deemed such a procedure necessary because of the increasing number of theologians who not only accepted the views of the critics of Christianity but actually joined forces with them.[4]

This apologetic method will be dealt with when we consider Warfield's systematic writings. We have mentioned it at this juncture to emphasize the continuity and discontinuity between Warfield and the former professors of theology at Princeton. Alexander and Hodge had contended against revivalists, Quakers, theologians foreign and domestic, and various speculative philosophies. They were professors of both polemic and didactic theol-

---

3. Livingstone, op. cit., pp. 112-133.
4. Ibid., pp. 149-51.

ogy which entailed not only defense but also attack. But their method, which depended on the use of the arguments from external and internal evidences, Warfield was to hone sharply into still another theological science—the science of apologetics. The sources of opposition were so numerous and enjoyed such widespread acceptance that he waged a full scale war as the only means of meeting the opposition.

However, as important as apologetics is in comprehending Warfield's thought, it comprises only one aspect of his thinking. Livingstone has contended that after the high water mark, as it were, of the role of internal evidences in Alexander's and Hodge's thought—especially in Hodge's *The Way of Life*—a remarkable drought characterized their successors' writings. In fact, he states, "any trace of subjectivity . . . was to vanish with Hodge's successors."[5] Undeniably external evidences and external authority assume a prominent position in Warfield's writings.[6] Nevertheless, internal evidences did not disappear from Warfield's thought. In his memorial address Patton emphasizes that Warfield stressed the presence of the Holy Spirit in the church: "He believed that over and above the external evidence in support of faith the individual Christian may have 'the witness within himself,' and that this subjective certitude is often a stronger support of his faith than any argument he can make."[7] One of the purposes of this chapter is to bring Warfield's continued use of such arguments into focus. Another emphasis will be to highlight his definition of religion in essentially subjective terms as dependence on God. A final emphasis of this chapter will be to show Warfield's preoccupation with various people's religious experience ranging from Charles Darwin's to Charles G. Finney's.

Unfortunately not enough material is extant to devote an extended section to Warfield's personal religious life. Apart from a few references by Patton in his memorial address and by Samuel G. Craig in the introduction to *Biblical and Theological Studies*, almost no biographical data remain at all. Robert H. Nichols in his article on Warfield in the *Dictionary of American Biography* rehearses his academic training and his abilities as a teacher but makes no references to his personal piety as he did in his article on Hodge.[8]

---

5. Ibid., p. 227.
6. Cf. Clyde Norman Kraus, "The Principle of Authority in the Theology of Benjamin B. Warfield, Wm. Adams Brown, and Gerald Birney Smith," unpublished Ph.D. thesis, Duke, 1961.
7. Patton, op. cit., p. 373.
8. "Benjamin B. Warfield," *American Dictionary of Biography*, 19: 453-54.

The following data are gathered from Craig's introduction.[9]

Warfield was born in Lexington, Kentucky, in 1851. Like Hodge he attended the College of New Jersey and graduated with highest honors in 1871. He was active in campus activities including debating and a campus magazine. Surprisingly enough, during his college years he was an ardent Darwinian and showed great promise in scientific pursuits.

The only reference that Craig makes to Warfield's early religious experience is his public profession of faith and his joining the Second Presbyterian Church in Lexington when he was 66 years old.[10] Whn Warfield went to Europe to study after his graduation, first to Edinburgh and then to Heidelberg, his letter home explaining a decision to enter the Christian ministry came as a surprise to his family. Although his mother had hoped that her sons might become ministers, Warfield had apparently exhibited no predilection toward studying theology. Craig states that it is not known why he decided to enter the ministry since "like his father he was ever reticent with regard to personal matters."[11]

After spending a year in Europe, Warfield returned to America and enrolled at Princeton Theological Seminary. Upon graduating in 1876 he returned to Europe to study at Leipzig, having married Annie Pearce Kinkead. He served as an assistant pastor in Baltimore in 1877 but resigned this position to accept an instructorship in New Testament at Western Theological Seminary. He remained there nine years before accepting a professorship at Princeton.

Patton's memorial address adds only slightly to this biographical sketch, but the following passage casts more light on his personality.

> He seldom preached in our neighboring cities, was not prominent in debates of the General Assembly, was not a member of any of the Boards of our Church, did not serve on committees, and wasted no energy in the pleasant but perhaps unprofitable pastime of after-dinner speaking. As was to be expected, therefore, he was too much of a recluse to be what is known as a popular man.[12]

Thus we have the picture of a scholar who lived with his books. Patton adds that his tendency to seek counsel from few people and his relative aloofness and detachment from people was "easily mistaken for haughtiness."[13] It is

9. "Benjamin B. Warfield," *Biblical and Theological Studies,* pp. xi-xviii.
10. Ibid., p. xiii.
11. Ibid.
12. Patton, op. cit., pp. 370-71.
13. Ibid., p. 388.

unfortunate that Warfield left behind no diaries or journals such as we found with Alexander and Hodge. Indeed, we have virtually no material other than his articles and devotional writings from which to get an impression of his personal religious life. While these are helpful and provide an insight into the character of his spiritual life,[14] this type of writing, even though dealing with the inner religious life, lacks the candidness and freshness of religious diaries. Such diaries and journals were invaluable in helping us see the intensity of religious feeling in the lives of Alexander and Hodge.

Conspicuously absent also in Warfield's case are the profuse references by his associates and friends to his own piety and religious life. While it is impossible to formulate an argument from silence, the absence of such material represents a formidable hindrance in our treatment of Warfield, particularly on the subject of religious experience. Since the main purpose of this study is to bring into clearer focus the emphasis that the Princeton men placed on this subject, this lack is compounded when it is compared with the amount of material available in our studies of the other two Princeton men and the insights they provided into their views. Since such personal narratives are wanting, the only recourse left to the interpreter of the Princeton theology is to compare the materials available with those of Alexander and Hodge. By comparing the systematic and devotional writings of Warfield with those of his predecessors we can infer similarities and differences in their personal religious lives. But it is only an inference that because the works of these three men on the subject of experience showed marked similarities, personal documents or reports of Warfield's family and friends, if they existed, would be similar to those of Alexander and Hodge. Nevertheless, since this is the only option open to us as an assumption, it will be used as judiciously as possible.

Warfield's Systematic Writings

When Warfield assumed the position of professor of theology at Princeton in 1887, he unequivocally delineated both his theological heritage and his plan to carry forth this tradition. He would continue the work begun so ably by Charles Hodge. The title of his inaugural address alone reveals the heritage he cherished: ''The Idea of Systematic Theology, Considered as a Science.'' He unabashedly announced his intention to follow his teacher's lead, and not simply in the content of the theology he would teach:

---

14. Cf. especially his ''The Religious Life of Theological Students'' treated below with his devotional writings.

> Though the power of Charles Hodge may not be upon me, the theology
> of Charles Hodge is within me, and . . . this is the theology which,
> according to my ability, I have it in my heart to teach to the students of
> the coming years. Oh, that the mantle of my Elijah might fall upon my
> shoulders; at least the message that was given to him is set within my
> lips.[15]

By mentioning the "mantle of Elijah" and asserting that "at least" the
content of theology will be the same, Warfield clearly expresses the hope
that other characteristics of Hodge might not fail of transfer. The remainder
of the address confirms this.

As the title implies, the speech is an explication of what systematic
theology is and how it presupposes man's ability to have scientific knowledge of God. If theology is the organization of the truth regarding God, three
things are presupposed: the reality of the subject matter, the ability of the
mind to comprehend and explain that subject matter, and a medium of
communication between the subject and the apprehending mind.[16] As for
the role of the religious feelings, Warfield points out that, while the natural
religious feelings indicate a dependence on God, theology demands objective truth as its basis. Without the "norm of Christian experience and its
dogmatic implication recorded for us in the perspicuous pages of the written
word" man would be liable to confuse what is merely human and what is
from God.[17] This means that the Scriptures are "the source of theology in
not only a degree, but also a sense in which nothing else is."[18] Statements
such as this are in direct continuity with similar assertions by Alexander and
Hodge.

But Warfield did not devote the entire address to a defense of the objective
foundations of theology. He asserts that the systematic theologian is not
simply an arranger of facts, propositions, and arguments. In fact this is not
even his primary responsibility. Preeminently he is a "preacher of the
Gospel." This means that his primary task is not to construct theological
syllogisms but rather to move men's religious affections. His vocation is:

---

15. "Inaugural Address," pp. 5, 6. The practice of looking back and praising one's
predecessors at Princeton was a common practice among the Princeton theologians. Cf.
*Proceedings Connected with the Semi-Centennial Commemoration of the Professorship of Rev.
Charles Hodge, D.D., LL.D., April 24, 1872;* cf. also Warfield's remarks on Hodge as a
teacher in *LCH*, pp. 588-91.

16. Ibid., p. 9.

17. Ibid., pp. 20, 21.

18. Ibid., p. 21.

. . . the moving of men through their power to love God with all their hearts, and their neighbors as themselves; to choose their portion with the Saviour of their souls; to find and hold him precious; and to recognize and yield to the sweet influences of the Holy Spirit. . . . With such truth as this he will not dare to deal in a cold and merely scientific spirit, but will justly and necessarily permit its preciousness and its practical destination to determine the spirit in which he handles it, and to awaken the reverential love with which alone he should investigate its reciprocal relations. For this he needs to be suffused at all times with a sense of the unspeakable worth of the revelation which lies before him . . . and with the bearings of its separate truths on his own heart and life; he needs to have had and to be having a full, rich, and deep religious experience of the great doctrines with which he deals; he needs to be living close to his God, to be resting always on the bosom of his Redeemer, to be filled at all times with the manifest influences of the Holy Spirit.[19]

It would be difficult to find even in Alexander and Hodge a better argument for the internal evidences of the Scriptures and of the Christian faith as a whole. This strong statement of internal evidence at the very beginning of his professorship is a clear indication that he intended to retain a primary emphasis of his predecessors. Whether he kept the two in quite the same balance as his predecessors is still to be determined. Before turning to this we shall examine Warfield's apologetic stance in broad outline and how it fits into his understanding of Calvinism. These subjects are drawn together in his explanation of Calvin's doctrine of the knowledge of God.

Livingstone has devoted his thesis to explaining Warfield's apologetic in detail. Nevertheless, we will note its salient points. Warfield's position can be fully understood only in light of what he considered the inroads that subjectivism had made in Christian theology. Apologetics is, in effect, a prolegomena to theology. As such its function is to guarantee the retention of Christianity's objectivity. Before the theologian can embark on his task he must be convinced of the three presuppositions of systematic theology which Warfield mentioned in his inaugural address. Apologetics clears the way for theology. For Warfield belief in Christianity is rational as opposed to irrational even though he admits as his predecessors had that demonstrations alone do not make people Christian believers. Therefore, Christianity as a system of thought is not a bald rationalism. Only the Holy Spirit can regenerate man's heart. But the Spirit does not work an irrational faith.

19. Ibid., p. 39.

> The Holy Spirit does not work a blind, an ungrounded faith in the heart. What is supplied by his creative energy in working faith is not a ready-made faith, rooted in nothing, and clinging without reason to its object; nor yet new grounds of belief in the object presented; but just a new ability of the heart to respond to the grounds of faith, sufficient in themselves, already present to the understanding.[20]

The principle on which this statement is based is that grounds for faith are present along with the creative act of the Spirit on the heart of the person. Therefore, apologetics has not only a defensive role to play to protect Christians from arguments of skeptics and to bring their head knowledge into alignment with their hearts; but apologetics has a primary part in the offensive Christianizing of the world. Indeed, Christianity's mission is "to *reason* its way to its dominion." While other religions depend on physical force, "Christianity makes its appeal to right reason, and stands out among all religions, therefore, as distinctively the Apologetic religion."[21] Apologetics establishes the objective validity of Christianity; it does not make people into Christians by coercing saving faith. Warfield continues to use external evidences in the tradition of Alexander and Hodge. But neither external evidences nor apologetics is sufficient to create faith in a person's heart. Only the Holy Spirit can do that. External evidences and apologetics perform the preparatory task of answering objections to the truth of Christianity. In effect, therefore, it establishes historical faith only. It accomplishes this not by taking individually the doctrines of Christianity and establishing them as true by appeals to reason. Such a procedure would be only to "transfer us at once into the atmosphere and betray us into the devious devices of the old vulgar rationalism."[22] Rather apologetics deals with those subjects which concern the essence of Christianity—i.e., God, religion, revelation, and the Bible. In assigning this as the task of apologetics Warfield does not leave any doubt as to what figures he is opposing by adopting this method. The original culprit was Kant who in effecting his Copernican revolution brought subjectivism to the fore in epistemology. Kant stated that while knowledge is based on evidence that is both subjectively and objectively valid, faith rests on evidence that is only subjectively valid.[23] In so doing Kant made knowledge the province of scientists alone.

---

20. Warfield, "Introductory Note," in Francis R. Beattie, *Apologetics or the Rational Vindication of Christianity,* p. 25.

21. Ibid., p. 26.

22. "Apologetics," *Studies in Theology,* p. 8.

23. Ibid., p. 14.

Faith was all that was left to the theologians. But Schleiermacher's theology is Warfield's immediate concern, since the German theologian replaced God as the subject matter of theology with the religious consciousness of the believer.[24]

Warfield articulated his most detailed explanation of objectivity and subjectivity in his article "Calvin's Doctrine of the Knowledge of God." In his careful explication of Calvin's thought, Warfield claimed his view was identical to the Genevan Reformer. His main concern is to show the relation between the objective and subjective elements in the knowledge of God and Christian truth. He begins with Calvin's assertion that man knows God in knowing himself. This knowledge is innate. But man's knowledge is affected by the subjective corruption of the soul. Therefore, man's innate knowledge and the knowledge acquired from nature are corrupted. God has revealed himself supernaturally in the Scriptures to overcome this corruption. This revelation is "attested as such by irresistible external evidence and attests itself as such by such marks of inherent divinity that no normal mind can resist them."[25] While the objective factor is fully established by this revelation, the subjective element in man is still in need of correction. This subjective corruption is overcome, however, by the "subjective action of the Spirit of God on the heart, by virtue of which it is opened for the perception and reception of the objective revelation of God."[26]

What Warfield is careful to emphasize is that, given man's corruption, neither the objective nor the subjective element is complete without the other. The testimony of the Spirit presupposes the objective Word and is not the revelation in the sense that the Word is. But conversely the objective revelation can have no effect on the human heart while it is corrupted by sin. When the Spirit restores man's spiritual sense lost through sin "the necessity of external proofs that the Scriptures are the Word of God is superseded: the Word of God is immediately perceived as such as light is perceived as light, sweetness as sweetness.[27] Thus, Warfield in fact retains the priority of internal over external evidence, Livingstone's claim notwithstanding. Warfield then launches into a 60-page explanation and defense of the testimony

---

24. Ibid. Cf. also "The Task and Method of Systematic Theology," ibid., pp. 96-97 and "The Idea of Systematic Theology," pp. 56-57.

25. *Calvin and Augustine,* p. 32. N.B. the presence of both external and internal evidences, and especially the apparent superiority of the former over the latter. Warfield later calls these evidences *indicia.*

26. Ibid.

27. Ibid., p. 33.

of the Holy Spirit. He contends that this is no isolated or incidental doctrine but is central to Calvin's thought because only that is true faith which the Spirit seals in the believer's heart. Objective proofs exist in abundance, which are sufficient of themselves to prove the truth of Christianity. Despite their cogency, however, they are incapable of producing saving faith.

> The knowledge of God which Calvin has in mind . . . is . . . a vital and vitalizing knowledge of God, and the attestation which he is seeking is not an attestation merely to the intelligence of men, compelling from them perhaps a reluctant judgment of the intellect alone . . . but such an attestation as takes hold of the whole man in the roots of his activities and controls all the movements of his soul.[28]

To indicate the subjective nature of the knowledge of God, Warfield emphasizes Calvin's contention that the testimony of the Holy Spirit is "in the heart."[29] It is "internal," "inward," and results in a "new spiritual sense" given only to God's elect.[30] In short, it is a perception or spiritual intuition "which comes only from divine gift." All of these factors indicate that Calvin's main purpose in writing of the Spirit's inner testimony is to give assurance to the elect.[31]

But what is the mode by which the Spirit testifies to the Scripture? It is not in the form of propositional revelation. In support of this he draws on Calvin's polemic against the Anabaptists. Quoting Calvin he states that the Holy Spirit's testimony is not to deliver new revelations but "to seal to our minds the same doctrine which the Gospel delivers."[32] Thus both the objective Word and the subjective work of the Spirit are the means by which the elect know God. The Calvinistic formula for describing the means of grace is the constant conjunction of the Word and the Spirit. The Spirit does not work apart from the Word, and the Word cannot produce faith without the testimony of the Spirit. The two are correlative. It is this Calvinistic principle that is at the heart of the Princeton epistemology. Livingstone, therefore, radically fails to understand this when he contends that the preparatory work of the Holy Spirit tends to be a *"deus ex machina"* to save

28. Ibid., p. 75.
29. Ibid., p. 76.
30. Ibid., p. 78.
31. Ibid., p. 79. E. A. Dowey asserts that the "question of certainty supplies the dominant motif in Calvin's doctrine of biblical authority, as well as his doctrine of faith in general" (*The Knowledge of God in Calvin's Theology,* p. 109). He cites several references in the *Institutes* which indicate that his preoccupation is to provide assurance to the elect.
32. Ibid. p. 80.

the Princeton theology from being a "rather bold rationalism."[33] The Scriptures and the *indicia* of the divinity of the Scriptures are objectively sufficient to compel man's reason to assent to their truth, but saving faith is impossible until the subjective deficiency in man is corrected by the testimony of the Spirit. Warfield is fully aware that Calvin disparaged attempts to prove to men the divinity of the Scriptures and the truth of both the Scriptures and the Christian faith. But this is not due to any deficiency in the evidences or the *indicia* involved.

But the point at issue for Warfield is whether the *indicia* and the Spirit work together in the same way that the Scriptures and the Spirit work. Since his concern is both to demonstrate the reasonableness of faith in the Scriptures and to deny that the Spirit's testimony is in the form of a revelation, he insists that the *indicia* and the Spirit work together. Such a juxtaposition of the two would assure that the reasonableness of Christianity preclude the identification of special revelation with the Spirit's testimony. Positing the two as correlative also proposes both an objective and subjective element, which preserves the traditional Princeton schema. His intention was not to raise the *indicia* "to a level of importance equal to that of the Scripture itself" as E. A. Dowey contends Warfield's position implies.[34] Despite Warfield's insistence that the *indicia* works with the Spirit in a way analogous to the working of the Scripture and the Spirit, he would have insisted that making the *indicia* equal in status to the Scripture would be to commit an error similar to that of making the Spirit's testimony a revelation. The Scripture was *sui generis* to the Princeton apologist, and neither the *indicia* nor the Spirit's testimony can claim to be the result of revelation and inspiration. Warfield asserts that the *indicia* and the Spirit work together not in order to elevate the *indicia* to a higher status but to assure the reasonableness of the Christian's faith at a time when such an idea was coming under increasing attack and to prevent the Spirit's testimony from being accepted as contemporary revelation.

Warfield states unequivocally that the *indicia* are incapable of producing saving faith. When the Spirit works in the soul to renew a sense of divinity of the Scriptures, it is "through the *indicia* of that divinity . . ."[35] Warfield

---

33. Livingstone, op. cit., p. 186, n. 118. In a more recent work Ernest R. Sandeen continues this criticism of Princeton in *The Roots of Fundamentalism,* (University of Chicago Press, 1970), chapter 5.

34. Dowey, op. cit., p. 116.

35. *Calvin and Augustine,* p. 87.

is forced to admit, however, that Calvin does not explicitly say this. In fact he is very careful to state clearly that Calvin actually seems to oppose this position.

> In treating of the *indicia,* Calvin does not, however, declare this [that the Spirit works through the *indicia*] in so many words. He sometimes even appears to speak of them rather as if they lay side by side with the testimony of the Spirit than acted along with it as co-factors in the production of the supreme effect. He speaks of their ineffectiveness in producing sound faith in the believer: and of their value as corrobora- tives to the believer: and his language would sometimes seem to suggest that therefore it were just as well not to employ them until after faith had formed itself under the testimony of the Spirit (I. viii. 1, 13). Of their part in forming faith under the operation of the testimony of the Spirit he does not appear explicitly to speak.[36]

While admitting this, Warfield contends that, while Calvin is not explicit on this matter, his position has *implicit* support in the general teaching of Calvin. Again Warfield cautiously avoids attributing to Calvin what is not in the *Institutes.* Therefore he states that Calvin stopped short of stating that the two work together because of "the warmth of his zeal for the necessity of the testimony of the Spirit which has led him to a constant contrasting of this divine with those human testimonies."[37] He then cites several passages from Calvin which assert that the *indicia* are ineffective until *after* the internal testimony of the Spirit works through the *indicia.* He states:

> This is already given, indeed, in his strenuous insistence that the work of the Spirit is not of the nature of a revelation, but of a confirmation of the revelation deposited in the Scriptures, especially when this is taken in connection with his teaching that Scripture is self-authenticating.[38]

He concludes by noting Calvin's illustration of the "sense of divinity" which the believer has in reading the Scriptures. The Spirit's working in the heart imparts this sense of divinity and divinity is sensed only where it truly is. Because the Scripture manifests divinity, this divinity is sensed by the

---

36. Ibid. p. 88. This passage is especially significant in light of another statement by Warfield regarding the expediency of adducing evidences to arouse *fides humana;* i.e., a historical faith: "We may argue, if we will, that it is not worth while to awake it—though opinions differ there: but how can we argue that it is a thing inherently impossible?" (Ibid., p. 125, n. 99). It seems as if Warfield, in recognizing that *indicia* can arouse only a *fides humana,* is calling into question the basis of apologetics. But he recovers to say that even though apologetics can only arouse a *fides humana* it is worthwhile. Though it does not save, it conclusively demonstrates that Christian faith is not unreasonable.

37. Ibid., p. 89.

38. Ibid.

believer prompted by the Spirit. When Calvin used the perception of light
and sweetness, Warfield insists that such things are perceived "by the
mediation of those *indicia* of light and darkness . . . sweetness and bitterness, by which these qualities manifest themselves to the natural senses."
Therefore, by analogy, states Warfield,

> we must accredit Calvin as thinking of the newly implanted spiritual
> sense discerning the divinity of Scripture only through the mediation of
> the *indicia* of divinity manifested in Scripture. To taste and see that the
> Scriptures are divine is to recognize a divinity actually inherent in
> Scripture; and of course recognition implies perception of *indicia*, not
> attribution of a divinity not recognized as inherent.[39]

It is to Warfield's credit that he admitted that such a teaching is only implied
in Calvin's thought. He conceded that Calvin's primary emphasis was on the
testimony of the Holy Spirit, and only secondary importance was accorded
to the *indicia*. Warfield's intention is to discredit the notion that the *indicia*
are insignificant.

The passages he cites from Calvin on the relationship between the Spirit's
testimony and the *indicia* do not support his position. It is clear from I, viii, i,
13 that for Calvin the *indicia*, while not separated from the testimony of the
Spirit, do not precede the Spirit but serve as confirmation. In the first
passage Calvin warns against the futility of using arguments to bring about
saving faith. Such arguments are better suited to confirm rather than to
establish faith.

> . . . once we have embraced it [the Scripture] devoutly as its dignity
> deserves, and have recognized it to be above the common sort of things,
> those arguments—not strong enough before to engraft and fix the
> certainty of Scripture in our minds—become very useful aids. . . .For
> truth is cleared of all doubt when, not sustained by external props, it
> serves as its own support.[40]

In the second passage Calvin asserts that excellent reasons can be given to
vindicate the Scriptures in the face of criticism by skeptics. However, they
are not sufficient of themselves to provide "a firm faith, until our Heavenly
Father, revealing his majesty there, lifts reverence for Scripture beyond the
realm of controversy." Calvin concludes:

> Therefore Scripture will ultimately suffice for a saving knowledge of
> God only when its certainty is founded upon the inward persuasion of

39. Ibid., p. 90.
40. John Calvin, *Institutes of the Christian Religion*, I, viii, 1, ed. John T. McNeill, 1: 82.

the Holy Spirit. Indeed, these human testimonies which exist to confirm it will not be vain if, as secondary aids to our feebleness, they follow that chief and highest testimony. But those who wish to prove to unbelievers that Scripture is the Word of God are acting foolishly, for only by faith can this be known.[41]

It is clear that a comparison of these passages with Warfield's position reveals that Warfield has exceeded making explicit what was implicit in Calvin's thought. Although Warfield distinguishes his position in its finished form from Calvin's, he has apparently reversed Calvin's understanding of the manner in which the two factors work together. Calvin states clearly that the testimony of the Spirit is the indispensable element but that the *indicia* perform an important confirmatory function. They are not mere appendages to his thought, subject to dismissal as either insignificant or irrelevant. Warfield, perceiving the integral role that the *indicia* play in Calvin's thought, in his zeal to retain them has gone further than Calvin not only by making the connection explicit but by making the *indicia* first in chronological order. This was due to his commitment to the task of apologetics, an exercise he considered necessary in light of prevailing theological thinking. While he accepted Calvin's insistence that arguments cannot cause saving faith, so portentous were the inroads being made by subjectivism and biblical and historical criticism in theological thinking, that he considered the silencing of skeptical objections not only worthwhile, but absolutely necessary. This is apparent from his insistence that the awakening of a *fides humana* is worthwhile. To contend that this enterprise is impossible is to assert that Christian faith is unreasonable. This, according to Warfield, is inadmissible.[42]

What Warfield does not seem to recognize is that Calvin was one who would have disagreed on the value of apologetics as a theological discipline. Even though he admits that Calvin contrasted the Spirit's testimony with human testimonies and that external evidences cannot produce saving faith and that it is foolish to enter into arguments, Warfield still engaged in apologetics. Undoubtedly one factor was that Warfield did not enjoy the advantage of being able to assume an historical faith on the part of his audience as Calvin did. Since Calvin could assume that the majority of his contemporaries gave at least intellectual assent to the Scriptures and the Christian faith, his task was to show how one gets from historical faith to

41. Ibid., I, viii, 13.
42. *Calvin and Augustine*, p. 125.

saving faith. Warfield obviously did not face such favorable circumstances. Since historical faith in the Bible and doctrines of Christianity could not be assumed, apologetics was designed to elicit historical faith. The role of the Holy Spirit was far from diminished, let alone deleted entirely from Warfield's thinking. But whenever an apologetic task is undertaken, the danger of degenerating into a mere rationalism is always present. Warfield's apologetic is no exception. Since apologetics is that discipline which precedes chronologically the task of theology, the theologian's *modus operandi* appears to be the accumulation and adducing of as many cogent evidences as possible for the truth of Christianity.

The underlying assumption, of course, is that the Spirit will work through them to produce saving faith. Such a program bears certain resemblances to the working of a "cause and effect" relationship and is obviously what Livingstone had in mind when he contended that the Holy Spirit tends to be a *deus ex machina*. But we must take full cognizance of Warfield's insistence that apologetics does not, in fact is utterly incapable of, replacing the Spirit's testimony. What gives rise to the suspicion of rationalism in Warfield's position is that in his resolution to retain the evidences he makes them precede the testimony. In Calvin both are integral to his attempt to give assurance to the believer, but the order is reversed; i.e., the evidences confirm saving faith, the latter being accomplished by the Spirit. The reason for the difference in Warfield's position is that he could not assume a historical faith, and his purpose in writing was to meet the objections to the Scriptures. Calvin's purpose on the other hand was to give assurance to the elect. Confronted with two such widely divergent purposes one should expect to find differences of presentation. What Warfield has attempted to do in effect is to show what, in his opinion, Calvin would have done had the circumstances been different. While certain implications adduced by Warfield are suggestive as to how the Reformer would have reacted to the absence of historical faith, such an attempt to imply that Calvin would have taken Warfield's stance, given the absence of explicit statements, is historically unsound. This is especially true considering Calvin's order of faith first, then the evidences.

Warfield's position resulted directly from his position as a supporter of a Calvinism that was losing the battle with the rising forces of liberalism. He fought both offensively and defensively for an orthodox position which he believed to be intellectually defensible. He could not allow the opinion to go unchallenged that to be a conservative was to jettison an intellectual approach to the faith. Therefore, while cognizant that the victory of an apologist might be a hollow one indeed, Warfield thought it worth the risk that men might be left with only an historical faith: at least there was hope that the Spirit would work through the evidences to convince the hearts of skeptics. Historical faith, then, was viewed as a kind of half-way house in the journey between unbelief and saving faith.

When speaking apologetically Warfield seems to advocate a two-step sequence in the knowledge of God. The first step is a historical faith in which a person believes *that* God exists. This is accomplished by means of apologetic appeal to rational argument involving the *indicia*. The second step is trust in God made possible after historical faith through the agency of the Holy Spirit. At other times, specifically when analyzing part of Calvin's doctrine of the knowledge of God, Warfield seems to advocate Calvin's position that knowledge of God is not merely by influence but is given as immediately correlative with knowledge of self-consciousness. Both elements can be found in Warfield and the presence of both indicates an occasional internal inconsistency to his thought. His desire was to be true to the spirit of Calvin. But the pressing needs of the apologetic battle influenced him to lean more upon the external evidence than Calvin did. No one seems to have known this better than Warfield himself, who acknowledged that the battle with unbelief required a modification of the great Reformer's position. The question to be posed, therefore, is how far did Warfield modify the Reformed position? Would his changes overthrow the balance his predecessors attempted to maintain between objectivity and subjectivity in religious experience? Nowhere was Warfield more explicit in his intention to maintain that balance than in his general definition of religion as dependence and his analysis of the psychological aspects of faith. To these two major elements in his thought we shall now turn our attention.

Whereas Hodge's most characteristic definition of religion was that it is a form of knowledge, Warfield never failed to emphasize that religion is essentially dependence on God. It was in his articles on Calvin, Augustine, and the Westminster Catechism that he vigorously defended what he considered to be the heart of the "Reformed consciousness," which originated not with the Reformers of the sixteenth century but with their great spiritual predecessor Augustine. It was the glory of Augustine that he brought about "revolution both in Christian teaching and in Christian life. . . ." The "new piety" beginning with Augustine is one in which,

in place of the alterations of hope and fear which vex the lives of those

who, in whatever degree, hanging their hopes on their own merits, a
mood of assured trust in the mercy of a gracious God is substituted as the
spring of Christian life."[43]

Of course corresponding to this piety was a theology that exalted the
unmerited grace of God. This doctrine and piety did not even originate with
Augustine in the fifth century but had its beginning with St. Paul in the first.
But Augustine is credited with rediscovering this emphasis for the church.
While Warfield criticized Adolph Harnack's analysis of some of Augustine's works, specifically the "Confessions," he noted that Harnack was
absolutely correct when he called Augustine the "Reformer of Christian
Piety."[44] Warfield describes Augustine's theology as the "earliest . . .
one of the fullest, richest, and most perfect expressions" of "evangelical"
religion.[45] Augustine's doctrine and piety manifest a remarkable correla-
tion. In his doctrine is manifest "his experience of God's seeking and saving
love toward a lost sinner expressing itself in propositional form"; in his piety
we can distinguish "his conviction that the sole hope of the sinner lies in the
free grace of a loving God expressing itself in the forms of feelings."
Augustinian doctrine and piety can thus be summarized in the simple phrase
"dependence on God."[46] Since religion is dependence on God, Augustin-
ianism is religion expressed in one of its purest forms.

   Augustine's spiritual descendant was Calvin, whom Warfield called the
"true successor of Augustine." And the essence of religion for both men is
their belief that religion is essentially dependence on God.[47] Man's relationship of dependence on God stems from a twofold truth—knowledge of
himself given in immediate self-consciousness and knowledge of that being
on whom he is dependent.[48] The most succinct formulation of this fundamental principle can be summarized as:

   a profound apprehension of God in his majesty, with the inevitably
   accompanying poignant realization of the exact nature of the relation
   sustained to Him by the creature as such, and particularly by the sinful
   creature.[49]

43. Ibid., pp. 320-21.
44. Ibid., p. 349.
45. Ibid., p. 348.
46. Ibid., p. 351. Cf. " 'Miserable Sinner Christianity' in the Hands of the Rationalists,"
Princeton Theological Review, 18 (1920): 270-73.
47. *Calvin and Augustine*, pp. 35, 323, 485, 487, 489. Cf. *The Westminster Assembly and
its Work*, p. 386.
48. Ibid., p. 35.
49. Ibid., p. 288.

The knowledge of God with which Calvin is concerned is not that of idle speculation but that which is firmly seated in the heart. This raises the essential requirement for the knowledge of God—piety.

Calvin's intention, states Warfield, is to awaken a practical knowledge of God in the hearts of his readers. He elicits a practical knowledge by arousing first fear or reverence and then trust. He awakens love by indicating that He is our Father. Both fear and love are the prerequisites of true piety, which in turn is the presupposition of saving faith. Reverence and love are not separated—they inform one another. Warfield quotes extensively from the *Institutes*, I, ii, 2:

> For until men feel that they owe everything to God, that they are cherished by His paternal care, that He is the author to them of all good things and nothing is to be sought out of Him, they will never subject themselves to Him in willing obedience. . . .
>
> Because he perceives Him to be the author of all good, in trial or in need . . . he at once commits himself to His protection, expectant of His help; because he is convinced that He is good and merciful, he rests on Him in assured trust. . . .[50]

That God is Lord quickens in man a sense of dependence; that God is Father excites man to love and trust in Him. While the emphasis on the divine sovereignty is commonly recognized as a focal point of Calvin's doctrine of the knowledge of God, Warfield contends that his doctrine is only fully apprehended when the divine sovereignty is seen as coordinate with the divine fatherhood. The sovereignty under which man lives and upon which he is dependent is the sovereignty of God our Father. Dependence naturally leads to trust because the Lord of the universe is also man's Father who loves man and wills man's good.[51]

In two short papers on "John Calvin the Theologian" and "The Present Day Attitude toward Calvinism, Its Causes and Signficance" Warfield reviews some of the charges that have been made against Calvin. To the accusation that the Reformer is guilty of intellectualism, Warfield answers that his theology is preeminently a theology of religious sentiment and that Calvin is the theologian who most clearly developed the work of the Holy Spirit. If ever a "theology of the heart" existed it was Calvin's: ". . . in him the maxim that 'It is the heart that makes the theologian' finds perhaps

50. Ibid., p. 174.
51. Ibid., p. 175.

its most eminent illustration.''[52] While Calvin's intellectual ability is manifest for any reader to observe, charges that he engaged in speculation on theological matters reveal a fundamental error in interpreting his thought. So great was his religious interest in theology that it instinctively restrained him from speculative curiosity. His treatment of the Trinity is one example of the caution he exercised lest he lose himself in ''intellectual subtleties.''[53] But nowhere is his restraint more evident than in his treatment of predestination. His interest in this great doctrine was not speculative but religious, and the focal point of that religious conception was not metaphysical probings but a soteriological concern. This soteriological interest reveals that at the heart of his thinking was one grand theme—religion as dependence on God.

> What was suffusing his heart and flowing in full flood into all the chambers of his soul was a profound sense of his indebtedness as a lost sinner to the free grace of God his Saviour. His zeal in asserting the doctrine of two-fold predestination is grounded in the clearness with which he perceived . . . that only so can the leaven of 'synergism' be eliminated and the free grace of God be preserved in its purity. . . . The roots of his zeal are planted, in a word, in his consciousness of absolute dependence as a sinner on the free mercy of a saving God.''[54]

Thus, even at that point where it might be thought that Calvin had actually succumbed to the temptation to engage in cosmic speculation, closer examination reveals that he was most religious. It was not his intellect but his heart that was in control.

The final point Warfield makes in this essay is that Calvin's soteriological interest led him to make what Warfield considered to be his ''greatest contribution to theological science''—the doctrine of the Holy Spirit. Not that others had not paid attention to the Spirit's offices. Augustine, for instance, in positing the work of salvation as a subjective experience understood it to be the work of the Spirit. But Calvin gave full expression to the role of the Spirit in salvation. He substituted the Holy Spirit for the church as the source of religious knowledge. Without the testimony of the Spirit man has no certain knowledge of God.[55]

---

52. Ibid., pp. 482-83.
53. Ibid., p, 483.
54. Ibid., p. 484. Warfield does not neglect to mention that other Reformers emphasized the sovereignty of God as if to infer that Calvin was the only one to emphasize this truth. He mentions Luther, Zwingli, and Bucer as others who stressed God's sovereignty. Cf. Dillenberger, John and Claude Welch, *Protestant Christianity,* pp. 34, 35.
55. *Calvin and Augustine,* pp. 485-87.

The address "The Present Day Attitude toward Calvinism," as might be expected, is not optimistic about the role of Calvinism in modern theological formulation. But neither is Warfield's address so pessimistic as to be the final eulogy of a once existent glory now faded. Warfield readily admits that hostile forces exist both in modern materialistic culture and in modern theologies which deny the existence of supernaturalism. However, positive indications are not lacking that Calvinism still has its adherents. Whenever Christians tenaciously believe the principles of Calvin in their hearts the spirit of Calvinism lives still. These are "humble souls, who, in the quiet of retired lives, have caught a vision of God in His glory and are cherishing in their hearts that vital flame of complete dependence on Him which is the very essence of Calvinism."[56] Such people exemplify in every aspect of their lives what is not only the dominant motif of Calvinism but its very lifeblood. This motif of dependence on God is exemplified in the soul's attitude in prayer. Prayer is the "religious attitude at its height." For most people it is but a momentary action. But the informing spirit of Calvinism impels the believer to maintain such an attitude even after he has risen from his knees. Warfield, therefore, defines Calvinism as the continuation of the prayerful attitude in all areas of life.

> Now, Calvinism means just the preservation, in all our thinking and feeling and action, of the attitude of utter dependence on God which we assume in prayer. It is the mood of religion made determinative of all our thinking and feeling and willing.[57]

If this is Calvinism, then the Calvinist "is the man who sees God."

> He has caught sight of the ineffable Vision, and he will not let it fade for a moment from his eyes—God in nature, God in history, God in grace. Everywhere he sees God in His mighty stepping, everywhere he feels the working of his mighty arm, the throbbing of His mighty heart.[58]

The Calvinist not only feels himself dependent but knows the Sovereign Father on whom he is dependent. The very knowledge by which he knows God and himself as dependent is God's gift through the Holy Spirit. The Spirit rivets his attention not in his own responses to God but on the divine grace itself. He "sees in every step of his recovery to good and to God the Almighty working of God's grace."[59]

---

56. Ibid., p. 496.
57. Ibid., p. 499; cf. p. 492.
58. Ibid., p. 503.
59. Ibid.

Warfield also developed his definition of religion as dependence on God in an article, "The First Question of the Westminster Shorter Catechism." Warfield adamantly opposed demands for revision of the work of the Westminster Divines. He credits the Shorter Catechism with preserving "the purity of the Reformed consciousness."[60] This consciousness is reflected by the high plane on which the catechism begins. The question concerning man's end draws his attention away from himself and his own salvation and focuses it instead on God and His glory.

Warfield uses the reference to God's glory to develop further his notion of dependence. While its primary connotation is passivity, inactivity does not exhaust the idea of dependence. Warfield develops an insightful analysis of the Reformed consciousness by showing that while the chief characteristic of the Shorter Catechism begins with man's glorifying God, it does not stop there. It also talks of man's active delight in God, and it sees the two as complementary, not antithetical.

The primary emphasis of the catechism is followed by an equally important secondary emphasis: ". . . man exists not merely that God may be glorified in him, but that he may delight in this glorious God."[61] Thus, declares Warfield, the "subjective as well as the objective side of the case" receives equal attention. Man is not just the passive object through which God is glorified. Man is also the exulting, delighting subject. Warfield's enthusiasm for this conception of man's delighting in God is spontaneous and unrestrained.

> Read the great Reformed divines. The note of their work is exultation in God. How Calvin, for example, glorified and delighted in God! Every page rings with this note, the note of personal joy in the Almighty, known to be, not the all-wise, merely, but the all-loving too.[62]

Then Warfield cites a passage from Augustine illustrating the same principle:

> "let God," he [Augustine] exhorts in another of those great sentences which stud his pages—". . . be all in all to thee, for in Him is the entirety of all that thou lovest; if thou dost hunger He is thy bread; if thou dost thirst He is thy drink; if thou art in darkness, He is thy light; . . . if

---

60. *The Westminister Assembly and its Work*, p. 379.

61. Ibid., p. 397.

62. Ibid. Warfield refers to the *Institutes*, I, ii. Similarly, in another article "On the Biblical Notion of 'Renewal' " Warfield stresses that even though the recovery of the doctrine of justification led the Reformers to stress the objective side of salvation, the subjective side was not thereby eliminated (*Biblical and Theological Studies*, p. 373).

thou art naked, He is thy garment of immortality . . ." (Tract, xiii, in Ev. Johan. 5). Delight in God, enjoyment of God—this is the recurrent refrain of all Augustine's speech of God; delight in God here, enjoyment of God forever.[63]

With this analysis Warfield's representation of religion as dependence on God is complete. What begins as the mere natural religious feeling is transformed into the hymn of exultation and delight of the renewed Christian heart. By ending on the brink of poetic praise Warfield displays the heart of Calvinist piety. The God on which the Christian depends is the sovereign Father who is both reverenced and loved. He is a God before whom the believer's whole life is lived in an attitude of prayer. To speculate on His nature beyond the limits of the Scripture is not only worthless but betrays the very spirit of religious dependence. Because salvation is God's gift, men cannot take heaven by storm. Finally, the Calvinist delights in God. He finds in Him his highest of enjoyments. Speculation, rationalism, and idle curiosity are so much mere trifling, if not vain pride, to those who rest in the divine will alone.

We shall now turn our attention to Warfield's discussion of faith. His enthusiasm for the idea of trust in the Lord was as spontaneous as his exultation in religious dependence. The two are closely related. His "On Faith in its Psychological Aspects" bears strong resemblance to Hodge's treatment of faith in his *Systematic Theology*. Warfield's obvious intention is to retain the objective content of faith. Therefore, he begins as his predecessors did with an etymological analysis of the word "faith" in several languages. His retention of Scottish philosophy is evident in his contention that faith has an element of compelled consent based on evidence.[64] Warfield echoes Hodge's criticism of Kant: "faith must not be distinguished from knowledge only that it may be confounded with conjecture."[65] In the instant one pronounces the grounds for belief to be objectively inadequate, they become subjectively inadequate as well. Likewise Warfield repudiates definitions that found faith on "subjective interest or consideration of value."[66]

Warfield then discusses the difference between knowledge and faith. He

63. *The Westminster Assembly and its Work*, pp. 398-99.
64. *Biblical and Theological Studies*, pp. 375-80. Another article entitled "Faith" in which much of this material on faith is duplicated with similar emphases is found in this same volume (pp. 404-44).
65. Ibid., p. 381.
66. Ibid., p. 385.

contends that reason and authority are involved in faith as well as in knowledge. What distinguishes the two is that knowledge is based on perception, while faith rests on belief in testimony. Since faith is the act of a rational creature, it is mere ''credulity'' to call faith unreasonable.[67] Assuming that faith rests on testimony, Warfield contends that what intrinsically separates faith from knowledge is the presence of trust in the former. He admits that faith underlies all knowledge to a greater or lesser extent. But when the two are contrasted, the element of trust is more suited to faith than to knowledge. Warfield sums up his view on the distinction between knowledge and faith thus:

> Matters of faith . . . are different from matters of knowledge—not as convictions less clear, firm, or well-grounded, not as convictions resting on grounds less objectively valid, not as convictions determined rather by desire, will than by evidence—but as convictions resting on grounds less direct and immediate to the soul, and therefore involving a more prominent element of trust. . . .[68]

While trust is present in every kind of faith, it is in *religious* faith that the essence of trust is most clearly manifest. Trust is in perfect harmony with Warfield's conception of religion as dependence. And what makes religious faith *sui generis* is that it is not content with ''mere beliefs of propositions, the contents of which happen to be of religious purport,'' but that it seeks specifically religious action, i.e., trust or dependence. Since it is the nature of trust to ''seek a personal object on which to repose,''

> religious faith reaches its height not in assent to propositions but in active trust in a person. Consequently, the element of trust is ''so prominent . . . when it rests on the person of God our benefactor, or of Christ our Saviour, as to absorb the prior implication of crediting almost altogether. Faith in God, and above all, faith in Jesus Christ, is just trust in its purity.''[69]

But just because faith has trust as its most prominent element, assent is not thereby eliminated. Trust implies a perceived ''trustworthiness in the object on which it reposes.''[70] Thus, Alexander's and Hodge's concern for the content of faith plus the role of man's subjective aspect is maintained intact by Warfield. He was no more a scholastic than the two former Princeton

---

67. Ibid., p. 388.
68. Ibid., p. 392.
69. Ibid., p. 393.
70. Ibid., p. 395.

professors. None of the Princetonians were scholastics demanding only assent to propositions. Man's intellect is active; but what distinguishes knowledge from faith is the same thing that distinguished historical faith from saving faith in Alexander and speculation from faith in Hodge. The writings of all three exhibit their intense, conscious concern to maintain both the intellectual and the emotional aspects of faith.

The final element in Warfield's discussion of the psychological aspects of faith is an attempt to show how faith is both an exercise of man's free volition in response to evidence and at the same time the work of the Holy Spirit. Warfield recognizes that many of the definitions of faith he repudiated as inadequate are attempts to do justice to man the acting believer. Those who have formulated these definitions assumed, however, that man can be responsible for his faith only if its source of action is man's free volition. Faith conceived in this way would seem to conflict with Warfield's insistence that faith includes an element of "forced consent," i.e., faith is a result of evidence that is perceived to be trustworthy. Warfield denies that since faith is based on evidence the mind is passive in believing and the individual is relieved of responsibility for his belief. Man's responsibility is heightened, not eliminated, when faith is based on evidence:

> Are we to hold that responsibility attaches to faith only when it does not rest on good reasons, or in other words is ungrounded, or insufficiently grounded, and is therefore arbitrary? In point of fact, we are responsible for our volitions only because our volitions are never arbitrary acts of a faculty within us called "will," but the determined acts of our whole selves, and therefore represent us. And we are responsible for our faith in precisely the same way because it is *our* faith, and represents us.[71]

Therefore, even though faith is the result of evidence, man is still responsible for it. But this raises the question of man's ability to respond to evidence. While the mind is not passive in believing, in order for it to respond to evidence, the subjective condition of man must be changed. No matter how adequate the evidence, the mind is unable to receive and respond to it until it is made capable of doing so. A mind unable to follow a mathematical demonstration is not convinced despite the full adequacy of the demonstration. Despite Warfield's use of mathematics as an example, which lends it a certain mechanical coloring, he is inflexible in his insistence that faith "is not the mechanical result of the adduction of the evidence."[72] The failure of

---

71. Ibid., p. 396.
72. Ibid., p. 397.

man to respond is due not to the nature of evidence but to man's subjective condition.

At this juncture Warfield returns to his emphasis on the work of the Holy Spirit. Only the work of the Spirit can heal the corruption of the mind. To avoid reaching this conclusion, many theologians have rejected the premise that faith is a rational act based on the evidence of testimony and have redefined faith as "an arbitrary act of sheer will, produced no one knows how."[73] Warfield, however, consistent with his definition of religion as dependence, states that faith is God's gift. But this gift is not given "in some mechanical manner" which would violate man's personality.

> The mode of the divine giving of faith is represented rather as involving the creation by God the Holy Spirit of a capacity for faith under the evidence submitted. It proceeds by the divine illumination of the understanding, softening of the heart, and quickening of the will, so that the man so affected may freely and must inevitably perceive the force and yield to the compelling power of the evidence of the trustworthiness of Jesus Christ as Saviour submitted to him in the gospel.[74]

While Warfield might be faulted for the heavy emphasis on the intellectual element by placing the effect on the understanding prior to that of the heart, it is to his credit that he has attempted to do justice to the fact that faith is both man's act and the gift of God.

Warfield then attempts to show the nature of faith as dependence and its relation to the evidence on which it is grounded. In doing so he considers the effect of evidence on man's mind in the unfallen, fallen, and renewed states. Since man is dependent on God, what distinguishes him from other creatures is that his dependence is not just an objective fact but a fact of his consciousness. Dependence in man's case is a self-conscious dependence. It is just this self-conscious dependence that is the very basis of man's faith. Self-consciousness is the active aspect; dependence is the passive aspect. But the manifestation of faith differs radically in man as unfallen, fallen, and redeemed.[75] In unfallen man the consciousness of dependence far surpasses mere assent. It rises above bare recognition because "it has a rich emotional result in the heart."[76] The sense of awe and reverence, while present, are overshadowed by love and trust. The spontaneity of loving trust indicates

---

73. Ibid., p. 398.
74. Ibid., pp. 398-99.
75. Ibid., p. 399.
76. Ibid., p. 400.

that this is faith in its purest form. In fallen man the expression of dependence is drastically vitiated. The sense of dependence is not lost, but it is utterly devoid of that loving trust which characterized unfallen man. Sin, in destroying the relation between man and God, renders loving trust impossible. Because fallen man can only look forward to judgment, trust deteriorates into distrust. Concurrently aware of his dependence on God, he nevertheless sets his face to be as independent as he can. Loving trust gives place to misery and hatred. Fallen man, therefore, is "not able to escape from his belief in God, yet [he] cannot possibly have faith in God, that is trust Him, entrust himself to Him.[77]

In his redeemed state what was lost in fallen man is restored. Redemption is God's act, not the sinner's. Because fallen man lacks both the objective power to earn God's grace and the subjective power even to turn to Him for grace, salvation must be God's gift. Salvation is not a *de novo* creation, but a renewal or restoration of that trust which existed in purity in unfallen man. Even though trust in renewed man is God's gift, it is not something contrary to his nature.

> It is beyond the powers of his nature as sinful man; but is something which belongs to human nature as such, which has been lost through sin and which can be restored only by the power of God. In this sense faith remains natural even in the renewed sinner. . . .[78]

Thus Warfield explains his contention that faith is both man's act and the gift of God. It is fully man's act in the renewed state because and only because God's grace has intervened. Apart from the work of the Spirit man knows his dependence but cannot exercise that act of loving trust which is correlative to his self-conscious sense of dependence. It is the fiducial element, made possible by the Spirit's regenerating power, that gives faith its characteristic element. But this fiducial element presupposes that knowledge of dependence present in fallen man though corrupted by sin. Therefore, Warfield can say that when saving faith is present, not just an intellectual element is present, but an emotional and a voluntary element as well. With the reemergence of loving trust faith is formed. For while the "central movement" in all faith is assent, it is in the "movement of sensibilities [i.e., trust] that faith fulfills itself. . . ."[79]

One final element indicating the extent to which the subjective element is

77. Ibid., p. 401.
78. Ibid.
79. Ibid., p. 403.

taken into account in Warfield's thought should be brought to light—the role of internal evidence. As we noted above, some critics have denied any subjectivity in the Princeton theology after Charles Hodge, specifically the presence of internal evidence. The explicit adducing of such evidence is not as prominent in Warfield's thought. But it is far from absent. Undeniably Warfield's description of the exulting and delighting Christian, his definition of religion as dependence, and his emphasis on the fiducial element in faith belie any charge that subjectivity is totally lacking. While he formulated no detailed exposition on the differences between internal and external arguments as did Alexander and Hodge, that he acknowledged the existence of both kinds of evidence is incontrovertible. Besides the two references touched on above, Warfield makes an explicit reference to internal and external evidences in his article, "Calvin's Doctrine of the Knowledge of God." The context is a discussion of the various confessions of faith that Warfield contends support his view of the *indicia* and the Spirit's testimony. The Westminster Confession is his main concern. The confession mentions the value of external evidence, which "induces us to a high and reverent esteem for Scripture." But the internal evidence is of greater moment. "The internal testimony of the characteristics of the Scriptures themselves is noted [in the Confession] and its higher value pointed out: They 'abundantly evidence' or 'manifest' the Scriptures 'to be the Word of God.' "[80]

Another example of his use of internal evidence is his article on " 'Redeemer' 'Redemption.' " While Warfield devotes a good portion of the article to an etymological study of these words and laments the tendency of modern theology to depreciate their original meanings, the theme of the article is a prolonged argument from internal evidence. The opening statement sets the tone of the piece: "There is no one of the titles of Christ which is more precious to Christian hearts than 'Redeemer.' "[81] The first several pages resemble a panegyric of the feelings. Warfield describes the effect that its mere mention has: "Whenever we pronounce it, the cross is placarded before our eyes and our hearts are filled with loving remembrance not only that Christ has given us salvation, but that he paid a mighty price for it."[82] He includes a lengthy discussion of the use of "Redeemer" in Christian devotional literature. Because it is a name "charged with deep emotion," hymn writers have used it extensively in devotional songs.[83] Phrases utiliz-

---

80. *Calvin and Augustine*, pp. 129-30.
81. *The Person and Work of Christ*, p. 325.
82. Ibid.
83. Ibid.

ing this precious word fill several pages and the list of authors who use it includes Shakespeare and Milton. He cites the Westminister Shorter Catechism as the means by which "from our earliest childhood the preciousness of this title has been impressed upon us."[84] The *Book of Common Prayer* utilizes "Redeemer" almost a dozen times. Thus, summarizes Warfield, "this constant pregnant use of the title 'Redeemer' to express our sense of what we owe to Christ, has prevailed in the Church for, say, a millennium and a half."[85] At the conclusion of the article Warfield laments the depreciation of meaning that "Redeemer" and other words have suffered. But his greatest sorrow is not the demise of mere words. "The saddest thing is the dying out of the hearts of men of the things for which they stand." He concludes with the challenge (the article was originally an address in the chapel at Princeton) to theological students to ascertain whether or not "Redeemer" stirs their own hearts. "The real thing for you to settle in your minds, therefore, is whether Christ is really a Redeemer to you. . . . Do you realize that Christ is your Ransomer and has actually shed blood for you as your ransom?"[86]

In light of the passages we have adduced, including Warfield's inaugural address, the charge that he abandoned the use of internal evidence is without foundation. He may not have explicitly used them as frequently as did his predecessors, but they are implicit in his writings on many subjects. Warfield's critics may have been prejudiced by his strong insistence on the necessity of apologetics as a theological science. Nevertheless, Livingstone's and Sandeen's charge that subjectivity is wholly lacking is irresponsible. Whether their statements are a result of merely overlooking the presence of internal evidences or are the result of a polemic against the Princeton theology is impossible to say. But a certain distortion of Warfield's theology has resulted from a lack of clear exposition of this element in his writings.

The final part of our treatment of Warfield's systematic writings will be devoted to his great preoccupation with different kinds of religious experience. So fascinated was he by the diversity of religious experiences that he devoted large segments of his writings to rehearsing the details of Augus-

---

84. Ibid., p. 327.
85. Ibid., p. 328. Warfield continues by showing that the Greek term Λυτρωτής originally had such an "analytical character" that it was not used devotionally. It was only after the "analytical edges had been softened a little by habit" that it found a wider acceptance in devotional contexts (ibid., p. 329).
86. Ibid., p. 347.

tine's, Jonathan Edwards's, Finney's, and even Charles Darwin's religious lives. Warfield provides us a written showcase, as it were, of various types of religious experiences. Except for his elaboration of the various kinds of mysticism, which extended beyond merely Christian mysticism, he limited his attention to various modifications of specifically Christian experience.

Warfield contrasts mysticism's main premise that religion is a matter of feelings in man to Christianity's presupposition that religion is revealed from God and is thus a religion of external authority. In "Mysticism and Christianity" Warfield claims that Christian mysticism does not differ in essence from natural religion. Since the mystic appeals to the feelings as his authority, his is not a religion that lends itself to conceptual expression.

> When he sinks within himself he finds feelings, not conception; his is an emotional, not a conceptual, religion; and feelings, emotions, though not inaudible, are not articulate. As a mystic he has no conceptional language in which to express what he feels. If he attempts to describe it he must make use of terms derived from the religious or philosophical thought in vogue about him. . . .[87]

Whether one's mysticism is naturalistic, pantheistic, or theistic, the material with which he works is the same in each case. Christian mysticism, therefore, has simply dressed the common phenomena of mystical thought in the garb of Christian language.[88] Warfield readily concedes that supernaturalistic mysticism "has the closest affinity with Christianity."[89] Supernaturalistic mysticism asserts that the origin of those feelings which provide one with knowledge of God are derived not from the natural religious consciousness, or from the "footprints of Deity" on the soul perceived by "quiescence and rapt contemplation," or from the identification of the soul with God. These are the respective positions of naturalistic, theosophical, and pantheistic mysticisms.[90] Instead supernaturalistic mysticism claims that the knowledge of God originates from the immediate working of the Spirit on the heart. Warfield acknowledges supernaturalistic mysticism's superficial similarity to evangelical Christianity's fundamental doctrine of the Holy Spirit. But supernaturalistic mysticism, despite its close resemblance, falls short of Christianity because of its tendency either to substitute

87. *Biblical and Theological Studies*, p. 447.
88. Ibid., p. 449.
89. Ibid., p. 450.
90. Ibid.

the believer's experience for the written Word or else to subordinate the Word to experience.[91] Either of these two alternatives represents a repudiation of the principle of external authority, which guarantees not only the objectivity of the Christian faith but also the soteriological element as well.

Warfield envisions the consequences of mysticism as a reversion to natural religion. In his opinion nothing is inherently wrong with natural religion. It is good in that its emphasis is on dependence and responsibility. But Christianity, while not abolishing natural religious feelings, fills natural religion with a soteriological content making it a religion suited to man as a sinner: "It does not supersede natural religion; it takes it up in its entirety unto itself, expanding it and developing it on new sides to meet new needs. . . ."[92] Mysticism, in contrast to Christianity, looks to the "God within." Its fatal weakness is that it is not an adequate religion for sinners. While it is adequate for those who are not sinners, it is not sufficient for men who are. Christianity offers Christ, and the Christian looks outward to Him and the cross rather than within.[93]

The mystical writers, rather than taking the historical facts of Christianity as "the very substance of Christianity," "sublimate [them] . . . into a mere set of symbols, a dramatization of psychological experiences succeeding one another in the soul."[94] Such writers "pass beyond Christ." In their opinion Christ is "but . . . a traveler along with us upon the common way."[95] This is the most reprehensible element of mysticism. It is an attempt to do away with forensic justification and imputed righteousness. Warfield quotes Evelyn Underhill to illustrate the mystical distaste for the Reformed doctrines of justification and sanctification: " 'nothing done for us, or exhibited to us, can have the significance of that which is done *in* us.' "[96] Warfield states that any Christian can make this statement but would mean something radically different from the mystic. The Spirit does a

---

91. Ibid., p. 451. Warfield mentions that at times the Scriptures and the Spirit are seen as coordinate. But because he has a tendency to see the issues in terms of "either/or" his consideration of the "coordinate" position is replaced by the other two categories of substitution and subordination. Livingstone rightly criticizes Warfield for failing to distinguish between those who essentially agree with him, differing only in details, and those who took radically different positions. By grouping both of these groups together he forced the former, who were quite orthodox, to join forces with the latter (op. cit., pp. 279, 280, 346, 347).

92. Ibid., p. 456.

93. Ibid., p. 458.

94. Ibid.

95. Ibid., p. 459.

96. Ibid.

work that is wholly new. He does not bring to life a dormant spark or innate spiritual life.

> The great thing about the indwelling of Christ of the Christian revelation is that He comes to us in His Spirit with creative power. *Veni, creator Spiritus,* we sing, and we look to be new creatures, created in Christ Jesus into newness of life.[97]

To the mystic, however, "Christ enters the heart not to produce something new but to arouse what was dormant, what has belonged to man as man from the beginning and only needs to be set to work."[98]

In another article reviewing four of Evelyn Underhill's books, Warfield expresses an obvious appreciation for the way in which they were written, i.e., "with a verve and enthusiasm which impart to it an élan . . . that sweeps the reader well-nigh off his feet."[99] Miss Underhill, states Warfield, has captured part of the essence of Christianity, but in so doing, has distorted it. In a sense Christianity is mysticism. One of Christianity's essential dogmas is that "God has immediate access to the human soul and that the Christian enjoys direct communion with God." Indeed, Warfield goes on to say "it is of the very essence of Christianity that it is in Christ that every Christian lives and that it is Christ who lives in every Christian."[100] However, lest Warfield become too enthusiastic for mysticism he cites criticisms of mystical thought from the Ritschlian school. In fact, he plays Wilhelm Herrmann's criticism off against mysticism and then turns the tables by criticizing Herrmann's thought by appealing to the modicum of truth which mysticism retains. Thus Warfield interprets mysticism and Ritschlian "rationalism" as two examples, at opposite extremes, of the tendency to find the truth within man rather than revealed from without. The following is an example of the way in which he uses Herrmann to criticize mysticism:

> . . . Herrmann tells the exact truth when he explains in well-chosen words that the piety of the mystic is such that at the highest point to which it leads Christ must vanish from the soul along with all else that is

---

97. Ibid., p. 460.
98. Ibid.
99. Review of *The Mystical Way, Mysticism, Immanence,* and *The Miracles* 12, (1914): 107.
100. Ibid., p. 122.Cf. "We may of course speak of a 'mystical aspect experience of the Holy Ghost' as 'the real truth of mysticism. . . . No man is a Christian who has not had the experience of the indwelling of Christ" ("Review of *Mysticism in Christianity* by W. K. Fleming and *Mysticism and Modern Life,* by John Buchlian, *Princeton Theological Review,* 14 [1914]: 347-48. Hereafter "Review").

external. ''When he has found God,'' he explains again, ''the mystic
has left Christ behind.''[101]

As an example of the explicit way in which Warfield plays Miss Underhill's
mysticism against Ritschl's ''rationalism'' the following passage might be
cited. He uses Miss Underhill's mysticism to attack statements that deny any
communion between the believer and Christ, and he uses Ritschlianism to
repudiate individual revelations to the believer.

> We shall not turn our backs on Mysticism therefore to throw ourselves
> into the arms of that Ritschlianism in which Miss Underhill, perhaps
> rightly, sees the most determined modern enemy of all mysticism. But
> neither need we in revolt from Ritschlianism cast ourselves into the
> arms of that Mystical individualism which would throw man back on
> what we have seen Miss Underhill speaking of as the ''revelations of the
> individual.''[102]

What Warfield has attempted, therefore, is to show that the two positions
represented by Miss Underhill and Ritschl are two examples at opposite
extremes of subjectivism. They differ not so much in essence as they do in
particulars. Warfield saw only a difference in temperament or ''tempera-
ture'' between the mystic and the rationalist. Both are subjectivists. The
mystic is hot, the rationalist cold. ''Warm up a Rationalist and you inevitably get a Mystic; chill down a Mystic and you find a Rationalist. . . . Each
centers himself in himself.''[103] Neither of the two positions takes sufficient
account of the historical facts of Christianity. The Ritschlian looks to the
ethical community and pays little attention to Christianity as a ''historical
religion.'' On the other hand the mystic takes the historical foundations
and makes them merely ''symbols of transaction'' occurring in the souls of
men.[104]

What is surprising is that Warfield seems more amenable to mysticism
than he does to rationalism. His considered opinion of both is that they are
simply different modifications of subjectivism. Each position assumes that
the source of authority is within man and not external. While he never states
that he would rather have one than the other, when all of the criticisms have

---

101. Review of *The Mystical Way* . . . , p. 122. Cf. *Biblical and Theological Studies*,
p. 459 for another example of the way Warfield plays these two elements against each other.

102. Review . . . ,'' p. 343. Cf. *Biblical and Theological Studies*, p. 452.

103. ''Review of *Mystik und geschichtliche Religion* by Wilhelm Fresenius, *Princeton
Theological Review*, 12 (1914): 338.

104. ''Review . . . ,'' p. 343. Warfield mentions pantheistic mysticism in *Biblical and
Theological Studies*, pp. 448, 450.

been made he acknowledges an element of truth in mysticism. In all of the articles quoted, Warfield affirms that every Christian is a mystic, but not every mystic is a Christian. In the article "Mysticism and Christianity" he states: "we would as soon have no Christ at all as the Christ Herrmann gives us."[105] And in the review of Evelyn Underhill's books he takes strong exception to a statement of Herrmann's to the effect that Christians do not have communion with the exalted Christ.[106] We have already noted one quotation in which Warfield strongly affirms that Christians have communion with God. Although it is an undeveloped area in his thought, he refers to this communion again in "Review of *Mystik und geschichtliche Religion* by Wilhelm Fresenius."

> There are multitudes of Mystics who are not Christians, but there is no Christian who is not a mystic,—who does not hold communion with God in his soul, and that not merely as the God of grace by virtue of whose recreative operations he is a Christian, but as the God of nature by virtue of whose creative, upholding, and governing operations he is a creature. . . . There is no Christian religion where there is no inward communion with God.[107]

It is clear that Warfield finds a greater affinity between mysticism and Christianity than he does between rationalism and Christianity, even though he considers both to be antagonistic to the fundamental principle of Christianity as he has understood it. In making these observations, we are aware that Warfield does not express his own theology in such terms. In the articles in which he treated these two modifications of Christianity Warfield meant to condemn the two extremes of subjectivist thought pervading theological studies, not to single out one for praise and the other for criticism. Nevertheless, an implied partiality toward mysticism is present due to Warfield's predilection toward, but unfortunately incomplete development of, the subject of communion with God through the Holy Spirit.

Even though Warfield does not develop the subject of communion with God, at least to the extent that Hodge does, his preoccupation with subjectivity is evident in parts of his writings. His almost devotional appreciation of Calvin's call for a heart knowledge of the gospel and his exposition of religion as dependence are evidences of a deeply felt appreciation for the role that the affections play in the theological task. As the final element in our

105. *Biblical and Theological Studies,* p. 459.

106. Warfield, op. cit., p. 122.

107. Warfield, op. cit., pp. 337, 338.

consideration of Warfield's systematic writings we will focus our attention on Warfield's engrossment with specific examples of religious experience.

We have already noted his appreciation for Augustinian piety. He devotes an extended article to the famous "Confessions." As an example of self-revelation of the human heart it is without equal in Warfield's estimation. In comparison he judges Jean Jacques Rousseau's "Confessions" worthy only of contempt. In contrast Rousseau's conception of self-revelation "rose little above exhibiting himself with his clothes off."[108] The major theme of Augustine's "Confessions," however, is not the life of the Bishop of Hippo, let alone the misdeeds of his life. As Warfield points out Augustine intended it not as a biography but as a theological treatise, the purpose of which was to glorify God and edify the reader. It is a theological treatise on the goodness of God. Augustine narrates his own personal experience "only as the most lively of illustrations of the dealings of God with the human soul as He makes it restless until it finds its rest in Him."[109] Warfield interprets the title "Confessions" in a "higher double sense," i.e., as a "confessing the grace of God and our humble dependence on Him, a sense compounded of mingled humility and praise."[110] Augustine's work is much more akin to John Newton's "Authentic Narrative" and John Bunyan's "Grace Abounding to the Chief of Sinners" than to Rousseau's "Confessions." Warfield even writes of the "poetic quality" of the "Confessions" that gives it not just character but "beauty."[111] Warfield uses the "Confessions" as an illustration of how Augustine's life exemplifies the principle of dependence on God's grace. Nowhere is God's grace more the theme of the "Confessions" than in the scene of his conversion.

> The human elements that enter into the process, or even into the act itself by which he came to God, only heightened the clearness of his own perception that it was to the grace of God alone that he owed his recovery, and he would have them similarly heighten the clearness with which his readers perceive it with him.[112]

Thus Augustine was Warfield's example *par excellence* of religious experience. His experience was the perfect reflection of the fundamental principle

---

108. *Calvin and Augustine,* p. 332. The main point of Warfield's criticism is that Rousseau's work was so shallow that one senses "an air of insincerity" pervading it and that it resembles a "picaroon novel" more than it does an authentic autobiography (ibid., p. 333).

109. Ibid., p. 338.

110. Ibid.

111. Ibid., p. 347.

112. Ibid., pp. 366-67.

of religion as dependence upon God. Piety or experience which did not magnify the grace of God was simply inferior. Any experience that exalted man's role in salvation did not sufficiently account for man's status as sinner saved only by God's grace.

Warfield did not write on Calvin's religious experience. But he commented briefly on the experience of Jonathan Edwards, the foremost American Calvinist.[113] Warfield admires Edwards's ability to maintain a balance between his spiritual development and his intellectual achievements. Edwards claimed that he made his salvation the primary interest of his younger years. Warfield's attention was captured by Edwards's response to the Scripture text I Timothy 1:17. The text became the means by which Edwards turned from a revulsion of the doctrine of God's sovereignty to a rejoicing acceptance of it. He quotes the same passage that Alexander did from the *Personal Narrative*. What struck Warfield was that from the time that Edwards was convinced of God's sovereignty "his understanding of divine things increased, and his enjoyment of God grew."[114] Warfield's high appraisal of Edwards is evidenced also in his respect for Edwards's role in the revival of the preceding century. Not only were few as qualified as the Northampton preacher to perceive the evil that often mixes with good in revivalistic excitement, but few took the precautions that he did.

> He diligently sought to curb excesses, and earnestly endeavored to separate the chaff from the wheat. But no one could protest more strongly against casting out the wheat with the chaff. He subjected all the phenomena of the revivals in which he participated to the most searching analytical study; and, while sadly acknowledging that much self-deception was possible, and that the rein could only too readily be given to false "enthusiasm," he earnestly contended that a genuine work of grace might find expression in mental and even physical excitement.[115]

Such an appraisal stands in stark contrast with Hodge's. This is not because Warfield was any more friendly to emotional excitement than was his predecessor. Had emotional outbursts been the focus of his attention, it is

---

113. Warfield was well aware that Edwards did not want to be known as a "blind follower of Calvin." The article from which the information on Edwards is taken ("Edwards and the New England Theology") was an attempt to show that Edwards maintained Calvinism at its best while the New England Theology was a "far cry" from Edwards's Calvinism. *Studies in Theology*, pp. 531, 533.

114. *Studies in Theology*, p. 521.

115. Ibid., p. 524.

probable that he would have been more critical in his remarks. His purpose, however, was to show the fine balance between the religious affections and intellectual acumen manifest in Edwards's thought. In fact Warfield eulogizes him for blending "the richest sentiment with the highest intellectual powers."[116] He praises Edwards for being eminently a man of faith. But his faith was matched by a "logical acuteness of the first order." This led Warfield to project the battle in which he was engaged, a full scale defense of Calvinism when it was no longer prominent, back onto Edwards. It is not difficult to interpret Warfield's comments on the New England theologian as indicative of the struggles in which Warfield was involved. He was far enough removed from the conflict between Princeton and the successors of Edwards that his comments on Edwards did not have the critical flavor of Hodge's. Hodge was too closely involved in a theological struggle with those who considered themselves descendants from Edwards and yet in his opinion had actually corrupted Calvin and Edwards.

Warfield's critical attention was taken up instead by the Oberlin School and various movements such as the "Higher Life" and "The Victorious Life" movements. This particular aspect of Warfield's thought is comparable with Alexander's and Hodge's confrontation with revivalism. Under the rubric "perfectionism" Warfield grouped the Oberlin School and other left wing movements. The connecting thread running through these various movements was the contention that sinless perfection is possible in this life. Although Warfield censured this motif, his criticism was not administered wholesale. He found much in Finney's revivals that witnessed an effective proclamation of the gospel. But for the most part use of the "new measures" and Finney's "imperious" manner eclipsed the good points.[117]

The doctrine of sinless perfection appeared in diverse forms. It is not necessary to examine in detail Warfield's criticism of the various forms to understand his position on the movement as a whole. The most serious charge he levels are that perfectionism violates the fundamental definition of religion as dependence, and perfectionism leads to a religious piety that

---

116. Ibid., p. 528. Another factor in Warfield's generally favorable description of Edwards in comparison with Hodge's attack in his *Constitutional History* is the disappearance of the tension between the Princeton men and New England theology. As mentioned in the historical remarks in the introduction, Warfield faced a completely different context historically from Hodge's. After the reunion of Old and New School factions in 1870 the Princeton antipathy to anything arising out of New England was mollified. Cf. Loetscher, op. cit., references in index, p. 193.

117. *Perfectionism*, p. 21.

severely devalues the conception of sin, i.e., it promises a perfection that is only subjective and not objective. Instead of dependence on God, perfectionism proposes a religion of works. Trust in God becomes a work rather than a passive dependence on God's grace: "Everywhere and always the initiative belongs to man; everywhere and always God's action is suspended upon man's will."[118]

Charles G. Finney's conception of the simplicity of moral action is singled out for special attention. In Finney's view the ultimate choice of good as the maxim for all other subordinate choices makes one sinless.[119] The weakness of this view is that obedience to the moral law is measured "not by the objective content of the law, but by the subjective ability of the agent."[120]

Against these deviations from Calvinism, Warfield poses the concept of dependence on God with its corollaries of forensic justification and imputed righteousness. The believer's justification is not based on his faith exercised as a work, but instead in God's work based on Christ's death and resurrection. Sanctification is complete only in Christ. Perfect sanctification, impossible in this life, is obtainable only in the future state. Warfield's criticism of perfectionist religious experience has its roots in an analysis of its faulty doctrine.

The most poignant of Warfield's narrations in his showcase of religious experiences is "Charles Darwin's Religious Life: A Sketch in Spiritual Biography." He draws on the materials in Darwin's "Life and Letters" published by Darwin's son. The "Life and Letters" was not published as a spiritual biography, yet Warfield believes that it contains enough relevant material to give a fairly accurate picture of the spiritual changes in the scientist's life. In Warfield's estimation it occupies a unique place in spiritual biography. Whereas in Augustine and Bunyan one finds a spiritual growth from darkness to light and in Rousseau a glimpse of an "essentially evil nature," in Darwin one can find a record of the "experiences of an essentially noble soul about which the shades of doubt are slowly gathering."[121] Warfield notes that Darwin's character was one of "unusual sweetness." He describes the scientist as "genial, warmhearted, generous,

---

118. Ibid., p. 348.
119. Finney's view bears striking resemblance to Kant's view of the Gesinnung in *Religion within the Limits of Reason Alone*.
120. Ibid., p. 146.
121. *Studies in Theology*, p. 542.

affectionate, good, just.''[122] Despite Darwin's denial that religious sentiment was ever well integrated in his personality, Warfield dismisses this as
the result of the ''leaven'' of his later years' turning away from religion. He
insists that a ''truly religious coloring'' is perceivable at least in his younger
years. But what Warfield senses acutely is the almost unnoticeable way in
which this sentiment declines in Darwin's life.

> . . . there gradually faded out from his thought all purely religious
> concepts, and there gradually died out of his heart all the higher
> religious sentiments, together with all the accompanying consolations,
> hopes, and aspirations. On the quiet stage of this amiable life there is
> played out before our eyes the tragedy of the death of religion out of a
> human soul.[123]

As evidence that religious sentiment was not totally absent from Darwin's
early life the Princeton apologist cites a passage which is strongly reminiscent of the testimony of Charles Hodge. Darwin states that he was often late
departing for school, but being a swift runner he rarely actually arrived late.
Despite his fleetness afoot, when it was doubtful that he would be on time,
he, in his own words, ''prayed earnestly to God.'' ''I well remember that I
attributed my success to the prayers and not to my quick running, and
marvelled how generally I was aided.''[124] Darwin's interest in religion
during his youth influenced him at one point to contemplate the ministry as
his profession. Upon examining the creed he found himself assenting to its
contents, but when faced with the question which the bishop asked of all
candidates, ''Do you trust that you are inwardly moved by the Holy Spirit?''
he expressed doubt that he could answer affirmatively.[125] He still expressed
his faith openly while on board the *Beagle,* as Warfield cites references in
Darwin's letters that he was mocked by the officers for appealing to the
Scriptures as an authority on moral questions.[126]

What is interesting in Warfield's description of Darwin's slowly declining
religious sentiment is the way in which he brings in other elements, which
recalls Hodge's linking of religious and aesthetic taste. One of the first
indications of the decline of Darwin's religious life is an ''atrophy'' of the
higher aesthetic tastes.[127] Warfield combines this aesthetic atrophy with

---

122. Ibid.
123. Ibid., p. 543.
124. Ibid., p. 544.
125. Ibid., p. 546.
126. Ibid., p. 547.
127. Ibid., p. 548.

Darwin's confession that evidences for Christianity that used to command his assent no longer did so. It took place during a period of ten years between the ages of 30 and 40. Darwin's treatment of the argument for the existence of God is mentioned and his testimony of the weight that the argument from feeling or devotion used to carry with him.

> The process that we have been observing, as has been truly said, is not that of an ejectment of reverence and faith from the system . . . or of an encysting of them . . . but simply an atrophy of them, as they dissolve painfully away. In Mr. Darwin's case this atrophy was accompanied by a similar deadening of his higher emotional nature, by which he lost his power of enjoying poetry, music, and to a large extent scenery. . . .[128]

This drawing together of aesthetic and religious elements is remarkably similar to Hodge's treatment of beauty. That Warfield should point to the decline of the effectiveness that the evidences for Christianity had for Darwin is quite predictable. But the inclusion of Darwin's "atrophy" of aesthetic appreciation of works of art and nature is somewhat of an unexpected element. Warfield never developed an apologetic for "beauty" such as we noticed explicitly stated in Hodge and in Alexander's writings. Nevertheless, the heavy dependence on this concept in the article of Darwin, the slight mention of "beauty" as characteristic of Augustine's "Confessions" and Warfield's own attempts at poetry[129] indicate that the aesthetic appreciation present in the preceding Princetonians did not fail of transfer in their successor.

Taking into consideration all of Warfield's accounts of the religious experience of others, it is evident that he uses them either as examples of what he considers true Christian piety (i.e., Augustinian) or as foils against which he shows the beauty of the concept of dependence on God. They are far more than an anthology of various kinds of piety. Only the piety which is traceable through Calvin, Augustine, and back to Paul fully exhibits the union between the objective and subjective elements constituting Christian experience. Christian experience is valid only if it is established on the bedrock of objective fact. Because perfectionism offers only a subjective sanctification, it is inferior to the Calvinist view of imputed righteousness. Such subjectivism fosters a "thin religious life"[130] which knows little of

---

128. Ibid., p. 577.

129. Warfield published "Four Hymns and Some Religious Verses" in 1910. The hymns were often used in seminary chapel services.

130. *Perfectionism*, p. 308.

intense spiritual struggle against sin. Because complete victory in some form
is expected in this life, perfectionism denies the Calvinistic doctrine of
perseverance, which emphasizes one's dependence on God. What little is
gained in the emphasis on obedience to and fulfillment of the demands of the
gospel in the perfectionist schemes is more than lost in the devaluation both
of sin and the definition they gave to perfection. The very fact that the
perfectionists qualify the sanctification actually attainable in this life is proof
to Warfield that Reformed piety is more faithful to the biblical perspective.
Sanctification is a process, necessarily incomplete in this life. The Christian
life, therefore, is one of constant warfare, of struggling with temptation.
Whatever victory believers have is the result of God's grace. Dependence on
God is as integral to Warfield's conception of the Christian life as it is to his
conception of the knowledge of God and salvation itself.

Summary of Warfield's Systematic Writings

The issues we have met in Warfield's systematic works have for the most
part been presaged in Alexander's and Hodge's works. Reading Warfield's
works would reveal little intimation that Calvinism was no longer the strong
force in American religion that it was before the disruption of the Presbyterian church in 1837. However, a careful examination of his writings
reveals a poignant element in his thought. This is nowhere more apparent
than in his article on Calvinism's contemporary status. Because of the
clamor for revision of the Westminster Confession he could no longer point
to the Presbyterians as the Calvinist denomination. His ultimate appeal is to
individuals who have "caught a vision of God in His glory." He poignantly
admits that the "fortunes of Calvinism are certainly not at their flood."[131]

Despite this decline of Calvinism and the decline of conservative theology
moving toward the confrontation between fundamentalism and liberalism in
the beginning of the twentieth century, Warfield maintained a staunch
defense of Calvinist theology and piety. His articles on various aspects of
Calvin's thought are very able and have not been given the attention they
deserve.[132] Those elements in his thinking which have caught the attention
of the critics are the apologetical ones. Some admit that he was no more of a
scholastic than were his predecessors, yet they do not cease to stress
Warfield's choice of apologetics as the vehicle to transmit Calvinism to the
modern world. Such a method was in keeping with the tradition that

---

131. *Calvin and Augustine,* p. 496.
132. However, Dowey, for example, implicitly admits Warfield's competence and the
value of his Calvin studies by the profuse references to his articles. Dowey quotes Warfield
more than any other source. Cf. p. viii.

theology was a science and insisted on the "aggressive" nature of Christianity. But it seems that Warfield has gone further than either the pastor or the theologian of Princeton. Warfield's claim that Christianity can "reason its way to dominance," his insistence on apologetics assuming the role of preparatory science conducted prior to theology, and his willingness to go beyond Calvin in certain areas (e.g., the role of the *indicia*) indicate that Princeton's detractors have some grounds for their criticisms. As in our treatment of Alexander and Hodge it has been our intention to indicate that an examination of Warfield's writings on religious experience reveals a subjective factor in his thinking that has been overlooked or ignored except for minor references. In summing up Warfield's systematic writings we will notice not only that Warfield maintained a position conformable with the Princeton tradition preceding him but also made some significant additions. These additions indicate that Warfield was not merely giving lip service to the positions of Alexander and Hodge. He was contributing his own thoughts as well, thus enriching the tradition passed down to him.

Warfield maintained the distinction between internal and external evidences for the divinity of the Scriptures and the truth of the Christian faith. While he retained this distinction and stressed on occasion the role of internal evidence, his strong preoccupation with apologetics gives a different impression from that of his predecessors. Historical faith was the inferior element in Alexander's and Hodge's writings. Whenever discussed, it was usually to contrast it with saving faith. The first two professors of theology at Princeton taught before the influence of biblical criticism was at its height. To a much greater extent than Warfield they were able to assume with Calvin the prevalence of historical faith. Hodge's writings especially were replete with references to America as a Christian nation.[133] Because Warfield could not assume this historical faith, he concentrated his energy on arousing it. Internal evidences, while not deleted, were more often than not subordinated to external evidences which could be buttressed with findings of the historian, the linguist, and the scientist. What was only the removal of preliminary doubts as the goal of external evidences in the earlier Princeton theologians became the full-blown preparatory science of apologetics in Warfield. While the goal was still fundamentally the same, the changing theological situation made Warfield give apologetics or the role of external evidences a greater emphasis. Warfield was not writing when the

---

133. Cf. "England and America," *Princeton Review* (Jan., 1862) and "President Lincoln," *Princeton Review* (July, 1865).

Calvinist flower in America was fading. For many the demise of Calvinism was an established fact. He wrote when conservative fundamental theology was pitted against the rising forces of liberalism. Thus all the positions that he took on theological issues tended to mirror the state of the conflict in which he was involved. [134] His position on internal and external evidences is but another example of the harder lines that conservatives were drawing due to the success of critical views and the decline of conservative views.

Besides internal and external evidences we have discussed the nature of faith held by each of the Princeton men. Warfield's analysis of the psychological aspects of faith is similar to Hodge's. However, it was in his analysis of faith that Warfield made his greatest contribution to the role that the subjective element plays in Christian faith. Both Alexander and Hodge had insisted that assent is essential to faith but that trust added the extra dimension that distinguished between mere historical or speculative faith and saving faith. Warfield retained this emphasis. Without a perception of the trustworthiness of the object of faith he insisted the believer is left in the throes of subjectivism. But Warfield made the element of trust a corollary of what religion is in its essence—dependence on God. It was the fundamental natural religious feeling. Calvinism, however, transformed this natural religion, and, with its emphasis first on the glory of God and second on man's salvation, made it the very center of its teaching. Calvinism did not abrogate the natural religious feeling but in transforming it brought it to its fullest potential. It is indeed unfortunate that Princeton's critics have chosen virtually to neglect this aspect of his writings.

However, as conceded above, the critics are not wholly unwarranted in stressing the apologetical nature of his work, for that was the cast of his writings as a whole. Nevertheless this emphasis on subjectivity fully informed all of their writings. The subjective element in Calvin enabled Warfield to claim that the Genevan Reformer's theology epitomizes religion as dependence on God. Despite all of his scholarly articles on textual studies in the Scriptures and defenses of verbal inspiration and biblical infallibility, these articles were but the prelude, or, in his own terms, the preparatory science of the theologian. The Calvinist theologian might rejoice both in the

---

134. The Princeton position on the inspiration of Scripture has been the most frequently cited evidence of the hardening which took place in the Princeton theology. While Alexander and Hodge were not so concerned about errors in the text, Warfield made it a central issue. He insisted that only a proved error in the non-extant autographs would be sufficient to establish beyond doubt that an error exists. Cf. Ernest R. Sandeen, "The Princeton Theology," *Church History* 31, (Sept. 1962): pp. 307-321, and Livingstone, op. cit., p. 271.

reasonableness of the Christian faith and one's ability to defend and establish its truth by the science of apologetics. But the Calvinist theologian glories most of all in the sense of dependence on God that is exemplified by the "religious" view of Calvin's *Institutes*. It was absolutely unthinkable, therefore, that Warfield could concede that Calvinism was dead. As long as one other heart existed which gave glory to God and rejoiced in its utter dependence on the sovereign Father of Christianity, the spirit of Calvinism was still alive. If he could find only a handful to whom the word "Redeemer" evoked the feelings of love and joy it was still worthwhile to defend the Calvinistic system of theology. It emphasizes man's sinfulness and need for salvation, and clearly states that salvation is wholly a matter of God's grace and not man's efforts. Salvation is based on the objective work of Christ. Man simply appropriates it through the work of the Holy Spirit on the heart. His faith is also man's act, and as such it is a reasonable faith. It is based on a perceived trustworthiness in the object toward which it is directed, and that object is ultimately the person of Christ. Man assents to the objectivity of His person and work and exercises loving trust in Him as a Redeemer. Therefore, Warfield retained the same relationship between objective and subjective elements in religious experience noted in Alexander and Hodge.

The final element in Warfield's thought which illustrates the continuity in the Princeton theology is his preoccupation with specific examples of religious experience. This was a peculiar interest of Alexander's as well. The latter's *Thoughts on Religious Experience* reads in part like a doctor's casebook of experiences. Hodge is relatively silent on this subject but Warfield picks it up again. He does not recount as many examples as Alexander did, and yet the Princeton apologist seems to have the same interest in recounting various examples of experiences for teaching purposes. Warfield delights in recounting the principle events of Augustine's life, Edwards's experience, and the boyhood experiences of Charles Hodge. When he recounts the spiritual experiences of Charles Finney or Charles Darwin, on the other hand, he uses them as examples of deviation from the Calvinistic pattern. From this showcase of religious experience we find that his attention was not solely focused on apologetics and the substantiation of the objective elements of the Christian faith. By narrating different examples from Augustine to Darwin and Finney he continued the Princeton tradition of piety coupled with doctrine. Because the two were so closely linked together it made little difference whether doctrine was discussed or conversion experiences narrated. What was of primary importance in his opinion was whether both doctrine and piety or experience were in accordance with the natural religious feelings of dependence on God. Doctrine was the objective and piety the subjective aspect of religion. To have the former reflect one religious philosophy and the latter reflect a diametrically opposed conception was inconceivable to Warfield. Augustinian doctrine and piety transmitted through Calvinism provides the biblical perspective of Christian experience.

Thus, Warfield's attempt to carry on the cause of Calvinism in the twentieth century included a continuing Princeton interest in the subjective element in Christian experience. He may have engaged in apologetics to such an extent that this element was practically relegated to a subordinate position at times. Nevertheless, it informs all of his writings in significant ways as our analysis has indicated. Those studies that have strongly criticized Warfield for his occasional deviation from Calvinism have erred by not pointing out ways in which he retained the strongly religious tone of the Reformer. Such critics should have called attention to his equally strong interest in religious experience and specifically the central role loving trust in a gracious God plays in all of his theological formulations.

Warfield's Devotional Writings

Despite the fact that Warfield was, in Patton's words, more of a "recluse" than his predecessors and did not preach extensively outside the Princeton community, as Alexander and Hodge had, several volumes of collected sermons exist: *The Power of God unto Salvation* (1903), *The Saviour of the World* (1913), and *Faith and Life* (1916). The first two contain sermons he preached in the chapel at Princeton and the third includes messages he delivered in the Sunday afternoon conferences in the seminary oratory. Although his sermons and devotional messages do not number in the hundreds as Alexander's and Hodge's do, yet a substantial sampling of his preaching remains in these volumes. We noted in the opening pages of this chapter that we lack numerous references to Warfield's personal religious life. The same is true for his preaching. However, Patton referred to his preaching in his memorial address. He states that Warfield's preaching voice was pleasant: "It had the liquid softness of the South" in comparison with "the metallic resonance of the North." As for manner, his public speaking lacked "the clarion tones of impassioned oratory." Instead, he spoke in a "conversational tone, and his sentences often closed with the suggestion of a rising inflection, as if he invited a hospitable reception from his hearers."[135] Patton's comment on the content of Warfield's sermons is that they were "models of the better sort of university preaching." He goes on to say, "they were the ripe result of religious experience and minute exegetical knowledge, and in their meditative simplicity reminded us of some of the best of the Puritan divines."[136]

Following the practice of the Princeton men who preceded him, Warfield stressed many of the themes in his preaching that he discussed in his more formal writings. This is especially fortunate for our study because his sermons contain several clear and unambiguous references to internal evidences, which we noted were somewhat less abundant in his other writings. They leave no doubt that Warfield made good use of internal evidences and did not appeal to external evidences for the truth of the Christian faith. The most striking example is the sermon, "Imitating the Incarnation," based on Philippians 2:5-8. Warfield compares the phrase "Christ our Example" with "Christ our Redeemer." To indicate how great a value "Christ our Example" has to the believer, he states that after "Christ our Redeemer" "no words can more deeply stir the Christian heart than these."[137] In Christ believers find "the moral ideal historically realized, and we bow before it as sublime and yearn after it with all the assembled desires of our renewed souls."[138] So compelling is the example of Christ's emptying Himself and becoming man in order to offer Himself as a sacrifice that after the desire to be "in Christ" the believer feels a "corresponding longing to be like Christ."[139] Paul's wording of what Christ has done manifests such an "eager spirit . . . and . . . loving clearness and firmness of touch" that these few verses rival the prologue in the Gospel of John as a "marvelously concise outline" of the essential doctrine of the gospel.[140]

Warfield's main point of the sermon is that the concept of God as a God of love so moves the hearts of men that they trust in Him. God's sacrifice of His Son moves man's heart. Warfield then shows by contrast the stark difference between the Christian God of love and the philosophical Absolute in their respective abilities to move men's hearts.

---

135. *Biblical and Theological Studies*, p. xvi.
136. *The Person and Work of Christ*, p. viii.
137. Ibid., p. 563.
138. Ibid.
139. Ibid., p. 564.
140. Ibid., p. 565.

We have and must have an ethical God; a God whom we can love, and in whom we can trust. We may feel awe in the presence of the Absolute, as we feel awe in the presence of the storm or of the earthquake: we may feel our dependence in its presence, as we feel our helplessness before the tornado or the flood. But we cannot love it; we cannot trust it; and our hearts, which are just as trustworthy a guide as our dialectics, cry out for a God whom we can love and trust.[141]

The fundamental idea of God as love is illustrated in its purity in the death of Christ. God is love, and His love is self-sacrificing. Since we are to follow Christ's example, we should model our own lives after this pattern of love. Indeed, the "life of self-sacrificing unselfishness is the most divinely beautiful life that man can live."[142]

In another sermon on "The Argument from Experience" Warfield, in speaking of the sinner's justification, asserts that Paul appeals to the justified sinner's experience. As evidence of their justification Paul appeals to the peace they have experienced. All of man's own efforts failed to produce this peace. The whole Epistle is designed to evoke a response from the justified sinner who has found peace at last. This response is called forth by "a loving presentation of the sacrifice and work of Christ."[143] Warfield calls this appeal to the believer's experience "an assault on their hearts." He cites Jerome who claims that Paul's words are not the ordinary words of men: " 'they have hands and feet'; they are living things and tug at our heart strings."[144] Such is the content of the Scriptures that its divinity is manifested, and Paul's very words stir the human heart in a way that assures the reader that they are not merely the product of human reason. In preaching on "The Glorified Christ" Warfield stresses that the mere mention of Christ's suffering death evokes a response from the Christian's heart. The suffering and death of Christ is enough to dispel critical doubt in the gospel: "Dimly seen through the ever-increasing obscurity of the gathering years, that great figure has still the power to attract the gaze and to quicken the pulses—yes, to dominate the lives—of men."[145] That Christians are children of God is taught by both Paul and John. While both teach the believer's sonship, Warfield focuses on John's subjective emphasis as opposed to Paul's objective emphasis. Whereas Paul speaks from the juridical viewpoint, i.e., our

---

141. Ibid., p. 571.
142. Ibid.
143. *The Power of God unto Salvation*, p. 78.
144. Ibid.
145. *The Savior of the World*, p. 184.

becoming sons by adoption, John focuses on the work of Christ within the believer. For both, salvation is a divine gift. But Warfield exults in the way that John states the matter.

> Elsewhere it is conveyed more didactically, more analytically; here it is conveyed emotionally. Elsewhere we are told that it came not of blood, nor of the will of the flesh, nor of the will of man, but of God; here we have the answering thrill of gratitude of the human heart at this unexpected, undeserved gift.[146]

In these passages internal evidences are primary. The particular subject under discussion by its very content so affects the heart of the believer that the heart recognizes it as coming not from man but from God. In some instances the reference is to the particular language in which it is couched, but more often than not reference is to the subject itself. Such is its nature that only God could be its author, and it speaks directly to the believer's heart arousing the religious affections. Even if we did not find any references to internal evidences in Warfield's more formal references, enough examples are in his sermons to refute Livingstone's contention that they are totally lacking.

That element which we noted as Warfield's most significant contribution to the Princeton tradition—religious feeling as dependence upon God—is constantly reiterated in his sermons. It is expanded and intertwined with the concepts we found so essential in Alexander's and Hodge's writings—contemplation and communion. In "Childlikeness" he uses the story of Jesus' blessing of the little children as a means for extolling the Christian life as a life of dependence. Not only were the children in the story rather small but they were literally "babies." Theirs was not even a conscious dependence. Their state was one of "helpless dependence; complete dependence upon the care of those whose care for them was necessary." He likened the babies to those who are a part of God's kingdom. God's kingdom is made up of "those who are helplessly dependent on the King of the Heavens."[147] In a sermon on "Prayer as the Means of Grace" Warfield picks up a theme we noted in his discussion of Calvinism, prayer as the epitome of dependence. The true attitude of the Christian is one of prayer because thereby he most fully acknowledges his dependence on God. True Christian teaching, therefore, will always foster the spirit of prayer. Since every type of teaching will produce its own peculiar kind of religious life, only that teaching which

146. *Faith and Life*, p. 453. Cf. also *The Power of God unto Salvation*, pp. 30-56.
147. Ibid., p. 78.

emphasizes God's sovereignty will engender lives that exhibit a prayerful attitude. Of course, Warfield saw this best fulfilled in Calvinism.

> For us Calvinists the attitude of prayer is the whole attitude of our lives. . . . it is the attitude of dependence and trust. But just because this is the attitude of prayer, prayer puts the soul in the attitude for receiving grace and is essentially a means of grace.[148]

In "The Way of Life" Warfield reminds his hearers that because God alone saves, not even faith has a causal role to play in our salvation. Since it is God who saves us we are dependent on His mercy alone. "Here are brought before us God our Lover, Christ our Redeemer, the Spirit our Sanctifier, as all operative in the one composite work of salvation."[149]

But the one sermon that stands out from all others on the subject of dependence is his "False Religions and True," based on Paul's address to the Athenians in Acts 17. His subject is Paul's use of the natural religious feeling as a point of departure for the presentation of the gospel. Man is naturally religious. What immediately strikes the reader in Warfield's development of this subject is the almost overwhelming similarity in expression between Warfield and Schleiermacher himself on the feeling of absolute dependence.

> Endowed with an ineradicable sense of dependence and of responsibility, man knows that Other on which he depends and to whom he is responsible in the very same act by which he knows himself. As he can never know himself save as dependent and responsible, he can never know himself without a consciousness of that Other Not-self. . . . How he shall conceive God . . . of that Over-not-self [sic] in contrast with which he is conscious of dependence and responsibility; how he shall feel toward God—that is, toward that Over-not-self [sic] conceived after this fashion or that; how he shall comport himself toward God, that is, over against that Over-not-self, [sic] so and not otherwise conceived, and . . . felt toward: these questions . . . raise additional problems. . . .[150]

In light of this particular means of expressing that truth, which was at the center of so much of his writings and yet was never expressed in quite this manner, it is not surprising that Warfield discusses Schleiermacher's conception of religion in more detail. His assessment of Schleiermacher is similar to Hodge's. The German theologian was led "by the laudable

148. Ibid., p. 151.
149. Ibid., p. 398.
150. *The Power of God unto Salvation*, pp. 232-33.

motive" of finding for religion an impregnable place where it might not be assailed on the "shallow ground of intellectualistic criticism."[151] Warfield explains that Schleiermacher called the feeling of absolute dependence an "immediate feeling" or an "immediate self-consciousness" in order to distinguish between feelings that result from perception of an object and feelings that are immediate and depend on no mediation. Religion belongs to the latter class and is thus freed from intellectual conception.

Schleiermacher's good motive of seeking to rid religion of criticism, in Warfield's opinion, has opened a Pandora's box in freeing religion from intellectual conceptions. What has proved to be the source of great misunderstanding is precisely Schleiermacher's "feeling of dependence." Since it is capable of being interpreted as simply an abstract feeling, the critic is justified in asking what religious connotation can be deduced from it at all. Warfield is perfectly content with the notion of religion as dependence. But it is dependence on a specific object—i.e., God. If the object is removed, the concept ceases to have any religious quality. In Warfield's opinion this qualification seems to have been intended by Schleiermacher himself.

> . . . he [Schleiermacher] distinguished between the feeling of dependence in general and the feeling of absolute dependence in particular; and on the supposition that absolute dependence can be felt only toward the Absolute, confined the religious feeling to it.[152]

But defining the feeling of dependence in this way, according to Warfield, is nothing less than a "subintroduction of the idea of God," which is in reality the "veiled admission that we have in this 'feeling of absolute dependence' not an 'immediate feeling,' but a feeling mediated by an idea, to wit, the idea of God."[153] This whole procedure just reinforces Warfield's contention that the quality of the feeling is determined by the objects on which they are focused, and that such a direct relationship underscores the primary place conceptions have in religion.

We have come again to the Princeton response to the theological context. Whereas Alexander's preoccupation was with the revivalist and confessionalist factions in the Presbyterian church, Warfield stands more with Hodge in strictly theological controversy in which the more dangerous of two elements was subjectivism.[154] Warfield's specific answer was that

---

151. Ibid., p. 238.
152. Ibid., p. 243.
153. Ibid.
154. After Hodge it is difficult to speak of the Princeton solution as an attempt at a *via media*.

religion as dependence upon God included both objective and subjective elements. The objective element is that "God," as the object of faith, has specific content. God exists and has revealed Himself in the Scriptures. The Scriptures provide for man's knowledge of God. Subjectively the Christian faith is the believer's loving dependence upon Him. Whereas Alexander and Hodge expounded the differences between historical and saving faith, Warfield's solution was to eulogize the feeling of dependence. In a sense he took the fundamental element of subjective theology—religion as dependence— reinterpreted it using the foundational principle of Calvinism, and turned it back on its opponents. What is particularly noteworthy is his somewhat sympathetic treatment of Schleiermacher himself. Like Hodge, Warfield praises Schleiermacher for trying to save Christianity from the skeptical doubts of the critics. But the truly remarkable fact is that, following Hodge again, he tried to show that Schleiermacher's religious life was better than his theology. Hodge did this by contending that while the German theologian's theology bore a striking resemblance to pantheism, his own personal piety or feelings were determined by his love for Christ which he retained from his Moravian background. Warfield's favorable treatment was due to his interpretation of Schleiermacher's practical reluctance to repudiate intellectual content from the feeling of dependence. In contending that the feeling of absolute dependence can be felt only toward the Absolute, Schleiermacher allowed intellectual content to reenter through the back door. Both Hodge and Warfield paid Schleiermacher a kind of backhanded compliment by saying he was not the subjectivist he could have been had he strictly followed his fundamental principles. Therefore, while they strongly denounced the kind of subjectivist thinking that was associated with the "Father of Liberal Theology" and lamented his introduction of it to the theological scene, they were not so caught up in polemics that they could not recognize what they considered redeeming features either in his piety or in his theology.

To return to Warfield's development of religion as dependence on God, it becomes evident that Warfield joined this idea with other themes familiar to us from Alexander's and Hodge's writings. What is most closely associated with dependence is the experience of communion with God and with Christ.

Besides Warfield's mention of the Ritschlian rationalism, which he interprets as a form of subjectivism, and occasional references to Catholic theology of mere assent in his discussion of Calvin, there are no opponents to the right of the Princeton position. Warfield's answer is essentially an answer to the subjectivism of his day. His contention is that subjectivism is not eradicated from Christianity but is always seen in a proper perspective.

In his sermons, particularly those sermons we mentioned above in our discussion of dependence, Warfield discusses the experience of communion, a theme lacking in his more systematic works. After discussing prayer as the primary example of the feeling of dependence, in "Prayer as the Means of Grace," Warfield develops the familiar thought that prayer is a means of communion with God. However, he adds an element we have not found before. He defines the primary idea of prayer as "communion with God, the meeting of the soul with God, and the holding of converse with him." We would assume that this is conscious converse. But we are unprepared for his statement, "God may have communion with us without prayer. . . . He may enter our hearts beneath consciousness, and deal with us from within; and because He is within us we can be in communion with Him apart from prayer."[155]

We are not told how to intepret this, for Warfield again picks up the idea of conscious communion and does not return to this "unconscious communion." The very possibility of unconscious communion with God is another of the undeveloped ideas in the writings of the Princeton men that tantalizes the interpreter. How close is such an experience to mysticism as Warfield understood it? In what sense is this experience communion when the believer is not conscious of it? The Princeton emphasis is usually that spiritual experience is rational and that the believer's mind is fully involved in experience lest it border on a mere imagining of the mind. God's mysterious *work* of grace in the believer's heart is often unknown to the consciousness of the believer, but it seems that "unconscious communion" does not fit into this category. It is not a matter of God's Spirit's working a work of grace but of communing. This whole concept is an intriguing yet incompletely developed element in Warfield's thought. But it indicates that Warfield considered the idea of communion to be an important one. The fact that communion can be unconscious lends a definite mystical quality to it.

In another sermon, on "Prayer as a Practice," Warfield again takes up the concept of communion. Although he does not explicitly state that he has Schleiermacher in mind, he devotes a large part of the sermon to a defense of two points which Schleiermacher specifically repudiated in his discussion of prayer in the *Glaubenslehre:* that man has communion with God in prayer and that prayer has an objective effect on God.[156] Warfield begins by

---

155. *Faith and Life*, p. 152.
156. H. R. Mackintosh in *Types of Modern Theology*, pp. 92-100, levels various criticisms of Schleiermacher's theology including his defective vew of prayer and the absence of a discus-

stressing prayer as the subjective act that follows one's apprehension of God. Prayer is not limited to mere petition but includes other elements such as thanksgiving and praise. His main point, however, is that prayer has an objective effect on God. "It terminates on God, and does not merely bound back like a boomerang upon our own persons."[157] But prayer also has important subjective effects on the believer who offers it. The first is the "objective blessings" the believer receives in answer to his requests; the second is the peculiar blessing one obtains from the very act of prayer itself—i.e., the blessing of communion with God, the "highest act of the soul"; finally blessings come to the believer because in the act of prayer he has assumed "the proper attitude of the creature" *vis a vis* God.[158] He calls the first purely objective while the other two are subjective, and he specifically mentions the second as the best illustration of the value of prayer.

Warfield does not explain in great detail the nature of this communion. He simply eulogizes the "purely subjective or reflex effects of prayer" as of the "highest benefit to us." Indeed Warfield calls communion with God in prayer the "very heart of the matter." It perfectly illustrates that end for which man was created—to glorify God and enjoy Him forever:

> . . . then man has attained his end, the sole purpose for which he was made . . . when he enters into communion with God, abides in His presence, streaming out to Him in all the emotions. . . . He who attains to this experience has attained all that is to be attained. He is *absorbed in the beatific vision*. He that sees God shall be like him.[159]

Thus Alexander and Hodge were not the only Princeton theologians who came close to expressing communion with God in phrases that have a mystical ring about them. Warfield alone uses the phrase "absorbed in the beatific vision." However, when communion is expressed in such terms Warfield would explain that he is suggesting nothing more than what he had stated regarding Christianity and mysticism. While not every mystic is a

---

sion on the consciousness of communion with God. "Not merely is the notion of our influencing God [in prayer] rejected firmly, on the familiar ground that there can be no interaction between creature and Creator; the writer keeps silent even on the cardinal subject of communion with the Father" (pp. 92-93). Regarding Warfield's major emphasis on dependence on God interpreted as loving trust, Schleiermacher is also silent: "*Childlike trust in God the Father*—this is a note he seems curiously unwilling or unable to strike." This latter omission is in Mackintosh's words, "the gravest defect in Schleiermacher's theology as a whole" (p. 98).

157. *Faith and Life*, p. 438.
158. Ibid.
159. Ibid., p. 439 (emphasis mine).

Christian, every Christian is indeed a mystic. The Holy Spirit has immediate access to the soul, and the Spirit is the means by which we have communion with God. But in his use of "beatific vision" he would have roundly denied any absorption of the individual in God.[160] Thus, the phrase has a specific Princeton interpretation.

In Warfield's devotional writings we have found the same themes we found in Alexander and Hodge. Although the dominant theme of all his writings is dependence on God, we have not found any rubric such as "beauty," under which he subsumed all of his various emphases, from apologetics to his avid concern for the mystical experience of believers. Nevertheless, the closest attempt to present such an integrated overview of objectivity and subjectivity appears in two addresses he delivered in the seminary, on the religious life of a seminary student. He delivered the first, "Spiritual Culture in the Theological Seminary," as a Sunday afternoon conference address on September 20, 1903. The second, "The Religious Life of Theological Students," he gave eight years later at the "Autumn Conference" of the seminary. In these two addresses Warfield attempted to bring together the two prerequisites of a good minister—godly living and a sound education—under the category of "vocation," a dominant Reformed theme. Foremost in Warfield's concern is the attempt to warn the students against a mere intellectual approach to their seminary education. He cautions the students against the danger of assuming the intellect to be the primary requirement for the ministry. A minister must be learned "on pain of being utterly incompetent for his work." But it is only one of the qualifications and is succeeded in importance by "spiritual fitness."[161]

But a greater danger exists than the assumption that intellectual instruction alone prepares one for the ministry. It is the tendency to establish a false antithesis between the intellectual life and the spiritual life. To Warfield "nothing could be more fatal" than playing one off against the other.

> Why should you turn from God when you turn to your books, or feel that you must turn from your books in order to turn to God? If learning and devotion are as antagonistic as that, then the intellectual life is in itself accursed, and there can be no question of a religious life for a student, even of theology. The mere fact that he is a student inhibits religion for him.[162]

---

160. Cf. "Spiritual Strengthening," in which Warfield discusses the indwelling of the Holy Spirit: "We are not transmuted into God; nor is God transfused into us so we become part of God" (*Faith and Life*, p. 277).

161. "The Religious Life of Theological Students," p. 1, hereafter "Religious Life."

162. Ibid., p. 2.

In the other address Warfield took a slightly different approach to the same error of opposing devotion and learning. If intellectualism assumes a position disproportionate to a student's religious life, the solution is not for him to disparage the intellectual bent but to increase his devotion. In a word, "there is not a too muchness in the case at all, but a too littleness somewhere else. The trouble is . . . not that [his] head has received too much attention, but that his heart has received too little."[163] With this common perspective in both messages Warfield suggests two solutions: he encourages the students to cultivate both learning and piety under the category of Christian vocation; and since the latter of the two was the more likely to be lacking at Princeton, he makes numerous practical suggestions for the students to implement in their personal religious lives to correct the "too littleness" of devotion.

The peculiar characteristic of religious study is that it provides the best opportunity for making work an act of devotion. With most intellectual disciplines, nothing inherent in the content itself can "feed the religious life, or . . . set in movement the religious emotions. . . ."[164] But with theology every aspect of one's study is fraught with significance. Since the object of theology is to make God known, all of a theologian's work brings the student into God's presence. Warfield applied this principle not only to the study of theology itself and biblical studies, but even to language study. The study of Hebrew was not just an exercise in philology. Word studies were to become religious exercises: "It is wonderful how even the strictist grammatical study can be informed with reverence. . . . Apply every word to your own souls . . . and never rest satisfied until you feel as well as understand." Indeed he could say that a student should approach every subject determined to "let nothing pass by . . . without sucking the honey from it."[165] The study of theology as a vocation or calling from God entails a devotional approach to the subject. Studies are religious exercises occupying not only the mind but the heart. In fact, he states, "they bring you daily and hourly into the very presence of God." Since the subject matter is God and His dealings with men, students should "put the shoes from off . . . their feet in this holy presence."[166] Of course, the danger still remained that such study could become "common." Therefore, Warfield sounded the

163. "Spiritual Culture in the Theological Seminary," p. 66, hereafter "Spiritual Culture."

164. "Religious Life," p. 5.

165. Ibid., pp. 73-74.

166. Ibid., p. 6.

warning that if the material became mere facts, "you are in danger of becoming weary of God."[167]

Thus one of the solutions to a disproportionate intellectualism was to view theological studies not as an end in themselves but as a means of religious devotion. Study of theology, languages, and the Scriptures ought never to be ends but means. Neither are they merely intellectual disciplines. Instead they are part of the student's religious vocation. Theological study is a specifically religious exercise. Even the most technical studies can assume spiritual significance. They serve not only the intellectual needs of man to know about God but become a kind of religious experience by which a student enters God's presence. Warfield could have pointed to any number of his own theological articles to illustrate this point. Whether his subject was Calvin's doctrine of God or an etymological study of "Faith" or "Redeemer," he fulfilled his own spiritual injunction to let nothing pass without "sucking the honey from it." We have noted in our survey of his systematic writings not only Warfield the scholar but Warfield the exulting believer.

But the concept of theological study as a religious vocation was only one part of the solution to the problem of a lack of devotion in comparison with one's academic training in theology, and it was the second element that occupied more of Warfield's attention. The first part of the solution still focused on the intellectual element although it was an attempt to mitigate the popular impression that theological training is merely an academic enterprise. In the second part of the solution Warfield dealt specifically with the cultivation of the religious life. Of particular note is the way in which Warfield includes some of the major emphases we have noted in the rest of his writings. When he expounds the purposes and advantages of organic worship, individual worship, Bible study, and devotional reading, he touches on the major themes of communion with God, meditation and contemplation, and the value of internal evidences.

In both addresses Warfield expounds the advantages of organic and individual worship. In advocating the former he stresses the opportunities provided by the seminary such as the chapel services and the Sunday afternoon conferences. Speaking as a faculty member, Warfield insists that despite his interest in the classroom with "mere parts of speech, or the significance of words, or the details of history, or the syllogisms of formal

---

167. Ibid., p. 7.

logic,'' his greatest concern is to "preserve a devout spirit and a reverent heart" among the members of the student body.[168] Therefore, he calls upon the students to take equal advantage of the opportunities the seminary offers to give expression to the corporate religious life. He encourages the students not to withdraw from such meetings. The health of the individual spiritual life depends on the students' participation in the organic life of the religious community.

> Nothing can take the place of this common organic worship of the community as a community. . . . Without it you cease to be a religious community and lack that support and stay, that incitement and spur, that comes to the individual from the organic life of the community of which he forms a part.[169]

Public religious life is one of the means of grace, therefore, which God has ordained to meet the spiritual needs of the individual.

But Warfield's stronger emphasis is on the individual religious life, indicating the deeply ingrained pietism he had in common with Alexander and Hodge. He did not hesitate to stress the believer's participation in the corporate life of the church, but his heart lay with the private life of devotion. In "Religious Life" he makes the organic religious life serve the individual. If a student does his part to promote the corporate life of the seminary, he will "draw out a support" for his personal religious life that is available "nowhere else."[170] But, he tells the students, the true "foundation stone of . . . piety" lies "in your closets, or rather in your hearts."[171] True religious devotion grows best "in seclusion and the darkness of the closet." In such an atmosphere the individual engages in communion with God.

> Let us then make it our chief concern in our preparation for the ministry to institute between our hearts and God . . . such an intimacy of communion . . . that we may see fulfilled in our own experience our Lord's promise not only to enter our hearts, but unbrokenly to abide in them and to unite them to Himself in an intimacy comparable to the union of the Father and the Son.[172]

The comparison of the believer's communion with God with the union between Father and the Son reveals Warfield's concern to distinguish the

---

168. "Spiritual Culture," p. 71.
169. "Religious Life," p. 8.
170. Ibid., p. 9.
171. Ibid., p. 12.
172. "Spiritual Culture," p. 76.

communion experience from mere contemplation. The Princeton men, including Warfield, wanted to make communion with God in prayer a meaningful spiritual experience—superior to meditation and yet not synonymous with revelation, which ceased with the apostolic church. All three Princeton men were very reluctant to describe this communion in any detail. To do so would present the temptation to attribute to it characteristics bordering on revelation.

Warfield explicitly places communion in a higher order than meditation. Meditation occupies some place between communion and mere thought, and it is almost as difficult to explain as communion. Its most important characteristic, which separates it from mere reasoning, is the religious affections associated with it: "it is reasoning transfigured by devout feeling; and it proceeds by broodingly dissolving rather than by logically analyzing the thought."[173] Meditation presupposes a familiarity with the Scriptures. His exhortation for students to learn the English Bible is reminiscent of Alexander's and Hodge's challenge to memorize the Scripture:

> You must taste its preciousness for yourselves, before you can apply its preciousness to others' needs. You must assimilate the Bible and make it your own, in that intimate sense which will fix its words fast in your hearts, if you would have those words rise spontaneously to your lips in your times of need, or in the times of the needs of others. Read, study, meditate . . . until the Bible is in you. Then the Bible will well up in you and come out from you in every season of need.[174]

The emphasis of the latter part of this passage exemplifies the Princeton insistence on the role of the Scriptures in the spiritual life of the believer. Not only does the Holy Spirit well up in the believer's life like a spring of water (cf. John 4:14), but the Word performs a similar function. In such imagery Warfield not only preserves an emphasis on the Scripture but combines the objective Word with the subjective function it fulfills in the spiritual life. The believer familiarizes himself with Scripture and memorizes it so that it becomes an intimate part of his spiritual experience.

In the address, "Spiritual Culture," exercises of the spiritual life are treated in descending order. Having first considered prayer as communion with God and contemplation of the Scriptures, he finally treats reading devotional literature. Several movements in the history of the church have produced literature eminently suited for spiritual edification. Mystical writ-

---

173. Ibid., p. 78.
174. Ibid., p. 79.

ings, evident throughout the history of the church and limited to no specific period, have certain characteristic marks—"a certain aloofness combined with a clear and piercing note of adoration."[175] Predictably Warfield included the Puritans as a source of devotional literature. Their writings are noted for expression of "intense devotion to duty and strong insistence on personal holiness." While the Puritan literary style is "unadorned," Warfield insists that when "the graces of style happen to be added to its clear good sense and profound piety, nothing could be more charming."[176] Warfield also mentions the evangelical movement of the eighteenth and nineteenth centuries and certain Anglican writers from the nineteenth century. He concludes that devotional writings suitable for edification come from all segments of the church and from all periods in its history. They range from what he calls the "Mariolatrous Romanism" of Thomas à Kempis and the "bald Pelagianism" of Sir Thomas Brown to the "penetrating mysticism" of the *Theologica Germanica* and the "plain evangelicalism" of John Newton.[177] What is common to them all is their unquestioned devotional appeal. Each one has "power in it to move and instruct the heart of whoever would live in the Spirit."[178] Finally, Warfield encourages his students to become acquainted with religious verse, prayers, hymns, and biography that have become famous in the history of the church. Even the creeds can be considered for devotional reading. Not only are they a deterrent to untheological devotion, they are examples of "compressed and weighted utterances of the Christian heart."[179]

Thus in these two messages to seminary students Warfield attempted to unite the two concerns we have found throughout our study of the Princeton theology. He has combined thorough theological investigation and piety of the religious life under the subject of vocation. In such an alliance he hoped to check a recurrent threat at Princeton of making the intellectual training the sole focus of seminary education. Warfield's thoughts at this juncture reveal a dual sensitivity. Like Alexander and Hodge before him, his theological writings reflect an interest in trends both outside of Princeton and within their own walls. External threats to the Princeton position from the left were calculated to be more substantial than those from the right. But close

---

175. Ibid., p. 80.
176. Ibid.
177. Ibid., p. 81.
178. Ibid.
179. Ibid., p. 85.

examination of the writings of these men reveals that they correctly perceived that within the Princeton fold itself the situation was actually the converse of what it was in the general theological milieu. Far from succumbing to the perils of subjectivism they needed to prod one another to recognize their peculiar proclivity in the opposite direction. For the benefit of those outside of Princeton Theological Seminary they denounced the evils attending the increasing subjectivism in theology. But privately they expressed a certain solicitude that within their own party the heart needed more attention. Not that they ever ceased emphasizing the role of the intellect and the primary importance of the objective element in religious experiences. But they were not so obsessed with the defense of objectivity that they did not occasionally recognize the dangers inherent in their own position.

These two addresses by Warfield represent an attempt to correct the problems internal to the Princeton theological approach. The one thing needful at Princeton was not a reprimand to students who had been remiss in their academic commitment. Far from it. Both speeches presuppose a disproportionate emphasis on the intellectual pursuits. Therefore, on two separate occasions Warfield not only cautioned the students lest they exercise the mind to the neglect of the religious affections, but gave explicit suggestions as to how they might bolster what was lacking in their piety and devotion. Warfield in continuity with his predecessors advocated a pietism to preclude the possibility of his position's degenerating into mere intellectualism. He retained not only the form of the pietism of his forerunners but the substance as well. In addition to the theology, he preserved the piety with its emphasis on communion with God, contemplation of the Scriptures, and the cultivation of the individual devotional life.

In assessing Warfield's writings as a whole, therefore, we find little that differs from those of Alexander and Hodge. Loetscher's comment that in Alexander's works is the ''germ''of Princeton theology is as valid for the writings of the Princeton trio on religious experience as it is for any other element in their theology. The historical context and the theological milieu changed radically from Alexander's inauguration in 1812 until Warfield's election to the chair of systematic theology at Princeton in 1887. And yet the Princeton theology remained virtually unchanged. Certain elements such as the defense of the Scriptures as infallibly inspired were tightened due to mounting opposition from without. Apologetics assumed a more prominent position, but the Princeton piety remained relatively unchanged during the nineteenth century. The objective element was the primary element not only in theology but also in experience. But the subjective was subordinate only in the sense that it had as its foundation the objective element. It was not just an irrelevant appendage. In all three men's devotional writings we have noted an implicit admission of the extremes to which an objective emphasis could lead, which supports our contention that the subjective element was not merely an afterthought in their theology. Their pietism was no ornamental addendum. It informed all of their writings. They meant faith to be more than intellectual assent, therefore, they insisted that the religious affections are a *sine qua non* of experience, and they intended their concept of communion with God to exceed the experience of contemplation of the Scriptures. Just as Alexander purposed to forge a *via media* between two extreme factions in the Presbyterian church, so Hodge and Warfield did not consider their views to be extreme. But no doubt exists that those opponents which they identified by name stood mostly to the left of their theological position rather than on both flanks.

This does not mean, however, that the Princeton men went to the extremes that some of their critics have implied and toward which some of their presuppositions influenced them. Even Warfield in taking the positions on the Scripture during the height of the fundamentalist controversy did not revert to a Protestant scholasticism. That the Princeton men did not achieve the ideal they constantly held before themselves of the relation between objectivity and subjectivity was not due to a conscious bifurcation of the two in theory. But their implementation of what was relatively well correlated in the abstract verged on a sharp demarcation when apologetic concerns came to the fore. Such occasions, which increased proportionately with the acceptance of critical views by more and more theologians, should not be permitted to eclipse the pietistic strand pervading all of their work. In their systematic writings is a continuing subjective emphasis with the same subjects recurring in each man's writings—internal evidence, the subjective aspects of faith, meditation on the Scriptures stimulating the religious affections, and communion with God, often expressed in mystical terms. No one can gainsay their attempt to balance the objective and subjective emphases. This is especially evident in their devotional messages addressed to their own followers at Princeton, where the tendency was to focus more on objective issues.

Two factors contribute to the impression that the subjective aspect decreased after Hodge: the disappearance from Warfield's writings of specific mention of positions to the right of Princeton's, and the increasing role

Warfield assigned to apologetics. With regard to the first, the clearest instance of a *via media* in the Princeton theology was Alexander's position. Not only definable positions existed to the left, but definable positions to the right as well. To the left were revivalists within the Presbyterian church. On the opposite extreme were the pure confessionalists within and the deists, Catholics, and philosophers without. With Hodge the situation was slightly changed, but an attempt at a *via media* is at least discernible. But references to those to the right were much fewer than those to the left until in Warfield they ceased almost altogether.

What is important, however, is that the Princeton theologians did not make a radical shift in their explanation of the nature of religious experience. This brings us to the second factor which gives the impression that the line on subjectivity was hardened. Undoubtedly, a hardening of the objective emphasis was proportionate to the increasing attacks made on the orthodox position. But Warfield did not proportionately *decrease* his emphasis on the subjective aspect of experience. The position on the Scriptures, for example, was tightened rather than loosened when the traditional view of inspiration was attacked. But Warfield did not cease emphasizing those subjective teachings that we found in both of his predecessors. He insisted on meditation and lamented the passing of spontaneity of the religious affections. The increasing importance of apologetics was not a change *in essence* of the Princeton tradition. Radical developments and above all the increasing subjectivism in theology were something over which Warfield had no control. There may have still been elements within the Presbyterian church and without that continued to insist on a bare assent to the Scriptures or a rational assent to metaphysical principles. But Warfield's attention was captured wholly by the struggle to the left because that was where the danger lay. In his devotional writings we found several warnings of the dangers to the right. He did not hesitate either to enumerate the dangers of an objective empahsis or to make typically pietistic suggestions as to how they might be overcome. And of course implicit and explicit in all of his writings from those on the fiducial character of faith to his comments on communion with God are warnings against making religion merely an intellectual matter.

In light of these factors no onus rests on Warfield for having betrayed any element of the Princeton tradition on religious experience. Not only did he retain the essential elements passed down to him, but he also made his own significant contribution in his interpretation of religion as dependence on God.

CONCLUSION

The Princeton theology exhibits both a strong objective doctrinal emphasis and an equally strong subjective strand of piety. The purpose of this study was to provide a corrective to existing expositions of the Princeton theology that have largely neglected the subjective element. While previous discussions have made passing references to the subjective elements in the writings of Alexander, Hodge, and Warfield, no attempt has been made to bring this element into clearer perspective. Instead the critics have focused their attention almost exlusively on the more dominant objective aspects of their theologies. Thus, the tendency has been to consider only one side of their thought.

In order to correct these interpretations the main emphasis of this study was the subjective element pervading not only their devotional writings, as might be expected, but their systematic writings as well. While not denying the objective complexion of their works, my purpose has been to demonstrate that the three professors of theology not only included both elements in their writings, but integrated them more successfully than critics have previously allowed. In either omitting or treating only cursorily, or, worse still, denying altogether the existence of subjective elements, the critics have done the Princeton men a grave injustice. None have explicitly accused Alexander, Hodge, or Warfield of reverting to scholasticism, but they have strongly implied that their tendencies were too much in that direction.

In establishing that the objective and subjective elements were held in better tension than was previously assumed, I have related several key subjective emphases recurrent in the writings of all three men to the objective emphases which other studies have already brought to light. This is not to assert either that certain discontinuities do not exist in their writings, considered as a whole, or that each man individually did not make his own significant contribution to these emphases. The historical note in the introduction stated that due to the span of time encompassed in this study certain changes in emphasis were to be expected. Such changes were most noticeable in Warfield's writings. But all things being considered, the most remarkable feature of the writings discussed is their striking similarity. This similarity is most evident in elements we have found recurring in all three men: internal evidences for the divinity of the Scriptures and the Christian faith; the subjective aspect of faith without which it would not be saving faith; meditation or contemplation of the Scriptures as a specifically spiritual experience; and communion with God, which at times assumed strongly mystical overtones.

While it is not my intention to summarize again the main points of each of these areas, it would be beneficial to notice that each one of the Princeton men maintained a tension between the objective and subjective factors. In judging the divinity of the Scriptures this tension is manifest not only by the existence of both internal and external evidences, but also by the adducing of internal evidences and the work of the Holy Spirit as indispensable. Underlying this discussion by all three men was the issue of belief in the Scriptures as man's act (intuition of its heavenly content) and yet God's act as well (the Holy Spirit opens one's mind to perceive the truth). Some critics in their interpretation of the Princeton theology paid exclusive attention to the role of the believer. Nelson, for example, claims that the perception of the divinity of the Scripture was only a function of certain romantic tendencies. On the other hand critics such as McAllister have stressed that the use of the Holy Spirit differed little from a modified rationalism in which the Spirit's function was described in cognitive terms, such as the Spirit's opening the eyes of the mind. But the subtlety of the Princeton position escapes both of these two extreme interpretations. The believer's perception of the divinity of the Scriptures is both an act of the exulting believer, who rejoices in the glimpse of divinity which he sees manifested therein much as he perceives God's hand in the created world, and a result of the regenerating power of God's Spirit without which man remains blinded by sin to the glory of God no matter where it is manifested.

The discussion of the objective and subjective aspects of faith in part involved the same issues as that on internal evidence. The issue here was how faith can include an element of forced consent and yet still be man's act. The Princeton men could have just parroted Scottish philosophy and made faith little more than knowledge of assent based on evidence. But they continually insisted that faith, while founded on an observed trustworthiness in its object, contains emotional aspects which make it man's act of loving trust. And it was specifically *religious* faith that best exemplified the fiducial aspects. In their discussions of faith they spoke to those outside Princeton on the left and to those within the fold on the right.

Contemplation of the Scriptures, as mentioned several times in this study, is a corollary of the argument from internal evidences. However, in contemplation or meditation the continuing nature of the act is paramount. Thus contemplation is more of an abiding experience than just a momentary perception or awareness. Contemplation was even described in terms which one might expect the Princeton men to reserve for the experience of communion with God. In fact these two experiences were often run together. Their view enabled them to assert that study of even the most mechanical nature could be transformed into contemplation simply by meditating on the spiritual significance of a theological subject or related discipline. The possibilities of experience that are open to the believer through contemplation served as a constant reminder that theology was an act of praise to God and not just a scholastic enterprise.

Finally, the experience of communion with God opened the broadest possibilities for expressing the pietistic strand that was the leitmotif of their writings. Considering their presuppositions, which demanded that they avoid any experience akin to revelation, inspiration, or absorption, the three Presbyterian scholars attempted to be as specific as they could regarding the nature of this experience. Each man used language exhibiting strong mystical overtones. Alexander's was the most erotic, but the other two men used such language as well. Hodge made the most successful attempt to explain explicitly the nature of communion with God. But the reticence of the Princeton men as a whole to go into greater detail about this mystical communion both tantalizes and frustrates the interpreter of their writings. Would their goal of perpetuating Calvinistic piety have been better served if, after describing communion with God, they had attempted to illustrate this communion with instances from their own devotional experiences? What examples could be cited from their own lives of "prayer as conversation" that distinguishes communion with God from mere contemplation of His Word? How in concrete instances does putting thoughts before the mind compare with the participation of the Spirit in the believer's life? As Warfield admits, mystical experience (and we can assume he means legitimate Christian mystical experience as well as other kinds) does not lend itself to conceptual explanation. The strong reserve characterizing these men with regard to their own experience is witness of this principle. Nevertheless, the interpreter senses that just as the word "piety" included many assumed connotations every time it was used, so was "communion with God" suggestive of experiences which, though an integral part of every Christian life, defy explanation. The Princeton men seemed to assume that their descriptions of and exhortations to the personal religious life were the limit of their calling. Going beyond description and exhortation by using examples from their own lives would be to give tacit approval to the practice of making any individual religious life a model, whether exhaustive or not, for others to follow. Not only could this lead to stressing the subjective aspect of faith, but it could lead to the more serious problem of spiritual pride. It could also lessen the role of the Holy Spirit working through Scripture as providing primary examples for the spiritual life.

Our investigation has revealed that despite the intention of the Princeton men to hold the constituent elements of religious experience in tension, they were more successful in theory than in actual practice. But their failure to carry through this relationship was due not to a conscious decision to cease emphasizing the subjective aspect but to circumstances in the historical and theological milieus which, in the Princeton men's opinion, necessitated an undertaking to bolster the tottering objective emphasis. It is this tendency in the Princeton theology that has captured the attention of the critics, and is, without doubt, the more prominent element in their writings as a whole. Although Warfield's case is the best illustration of a response to the mounting number of issues in Princeton's theology that were coming under attack, the same is relatively true for both of his predecessors. In each instance, as the debate grew, whether it concerned the decline of Calvinism in the first half of the nineteenth century, or the rising debate between fundamentalism and liberalism in the twentieth, the Princeton men responded by stressing the objective elements in theology and experience to counteract what they considered to be either increasing subjectivism or claims attacking the Christian faith. It is only in this sense that subjective elements received less attention. The failure is relative, not absolute.

In light of these elements perhaps the most that can be said concerning the disproportionate emphasis on objectivity over subjectivity in the Princeton writings is a statement by Loetscher in *The Broadening Church*. He states that while the Princeton men ''had a depth of piety and of spiritual experience'' and while the Princeton theology itself had ''many widely recognized merits,'' it ''did not fully do justice to itself.''[1] But admitting that the Princeton theology failed to ''do justice to itself'' does not invalidate the major purpose in this study—to set in bolder relief the pietistic strand that informs the writings of these men. Not only is this subjective element present, but the omission of it renders the interpretations of their thought as a

---

1. Frederick Wm. Loetscher, *The Broadening Church* (Philadelphia: University of Pennsylvania Press, 1954), p. 22.

whole radically incomplete. Had the theological milieu been different their approach might have exhibited an entirely different emphasis. Nevertheless, their theological writings represent a conscious attempt to preserve the tradition which came down to them. With their predilection toward objectivity they could have reverted to scholasticism. But they did not. Instead they attempted to perpetuate a theology and a piety that were correlative in all respects—a theology to inform and instruct the intellect and a piety to fill and motivate the heart. Both theology and piety were to glorify God.

BIBLIOGRAPHY

Primary Sources

ARCHIBALD ALEXANDER

A Brief Outline of the Evidences of the Christian Religion. Philadelphia: American Sunday School Union, 1829.

"Communion—The Difference between Christian and Church Fellowship, and between Communion and its Symbols." *The Biblical Repertory and Princeton Review* 22 (1850).

"Dr. Alexander's Sermons Nov. 7 – Sept. 26, 1817," unpublished notes taken by Charles Hodge while a student at Princeton Seminary.

"Enthusiasm and Fanaticism." Unpublished manuscript (hereafter indicated ms.).

Evidences of the Authenticity, Inspiration, and Canonical Authority of the Holy Scriptures. Philadelphia: J. Whitham and Son, 1842.

"Evidences of a New Heart." *Biblical Repertory and Theological Review* 6, no. 3 (1834).

"Farewell Sermon . . . upon Leaving Philadelphia for Princeton," ms.

"Funeral Sermon Occasioned by the Decease of Samuel Miller," ms.

"Inaugural Discourse," privately printed, n.d.

"Journal, Oct. 1 – Dec. 31, 1791," ms.

"Justification by Faith, the Cardinal Doctrine of the Scriptures and of the Reformation," New York: American Tract Society, n.d.

"Lectures on Didactic Theology," ms.

"Letter" in *Lectures on Revivals of Religion,* William B. Sprague. New York: Webster & Skinners, Albany, 1832.

"Letters to Charles Hodge," ms.

"Love to an Unseen Saviour." Philadelphia: Presbyterian Board of Publication, n.d.

"Missionary Sermon."

"On the Nature of Vital Piety," introductory essay to *Advice to a Young Christian,* Jared Waterbury. New York: Robert Carter, 1848.

Outlines of Moral Science. New York: Charles Scribner's Sons, 1871.

Practical Sermons: to be Read in Families and Social Meetings. Philadelphia: Presbyterian Board of Publication, 1850.

Practical Truths. New York: American Tract Society, n.d.

"Practical View of Regeneration." *Biblical Repertory and Theological Review* 8, no. 4, (1836).

A Rational Defense of the Gospel, Isaac Watts, preface by Archibald Alexander. New York: Jonathan Leavitt, 1831.

A Selection of Hymns, Adapted to the Devotions of the Closet, the Family and the Social Circle; and Containing Subjects Appropriate to the Monthly Concerts of Prayer for the Success of Missions and Sunday Schools; and other Special Occasions. New York: Jonathan Leavitt, 1831.

"Sermon on the Character of the Rev. N. Legrand," ms.

"Sermons," ms.

"A System of Theology," ms.

Thoughts on Religious Experience. Philadelphia: Presbyterian Board of Publications, 1844.

"A Treatise in which the Difference between a Living and a Dead Faith is Explained, April, 1791," ms.

"The Way of Salvation Familiarly Explained, in a Conversation between a Father and His Children." Philadelphia: Presbyterian Board of Publications, 1839.

CHARLES HODGE

"Address at His Semicentennial Celebration in Princeton, 1872," ms.

"A Brief Account of the Last Hours of Albert B. Dod, Nov. 20, 1845." John T. Robinson, n.d.

"By One Spirit We Are All Baptized into One Body," ms.

Conference Papers. New York: Charles Scribner's Sons, 1879.

The Constitutional History of the Presbyterian Church in the United States of America. Philadelphia: Presbyterian Board of Education, 1840.

"A Discourse Delivered at the Re-Opening of the Chapel, Sept. 27, 1874," Princeton, 1874.

"Discourse on Christian Nurture." *Biblical Repertory and Princeton Review* 19, no. 4, (1847).

"Early Sermons, undated," ms.

"England and America." *Princeton Review,* Jan. 1862.

"The Faithful Mother's Reward," intro. by Charles Hodge, Philadelphia: Presbyterian Board of Education, 1833.

"Five Early Sermons," ms.

"Journal of European Travels, Feb. 1827 – April, 1828," ms.

"Lecture Addressed to the Students of the Theological Seminary, Nov. 7, 1828," ms.

"Lecture Notes on Systematic Theology," ms.

"Memoir of Dr. Alexander." *Biblical Repertory and Princeton Review* 27, no. 1, p. 151.

"Memoranda and Lecture Notes," ms.

"Miscellaneous Talks and Sermons for Baptisms, Ordinations, Funerals, etc.," ms.

"Notes on Lectures by Charles Hodge Written by C. W. Hodge and Classmate," ms.

"The Place of the Bible in a System of Education," American Sunday School Union, n.d.

"President Lincoln." *Princeton Review*. July, 1865.

Proceedings Connected with the Semi-Centennial Commemoration of the Professorship of Rev. Charles Hodge, D.D., LL.D., April 24, 1872. New York: Anson D. F. Randolph and Co., 1872.

"Proper Method of Dealing with Inquirers." American Tract Society, 1876.

"Regeneration." *Biblical Repertory and Theological Review* 2, no. 2, (1830).

"Review of Sprague's Lectures to Young People." *Biblical Repertory and Theological Review* 3, no. 3, 1831.

"Sermons," ms.

"Sermons New Series #1-47 Preached and Repreached between 1842-1876," ms.

"Sermons Preached and Repreached between 1825-1874," ms.

"Suggestions to Theological Students, on Some of those Traits of Character, which the Spirit of the Age Renders Peculiarly Important in the Ministers of the Gospel." *Biblical Repertory and Theological Review* 5, no. 1, (1833).

Systematic Theology. London: James Clarke & Co., 1960.

"The Theology of the Intellect and that of the Feelings." *Biblical Repertory and Princeton Review* 22, no. 4 (1850).

"Transcript of Letters Sent to Charles Hodge by Various Friends between 1827-1842," ms.

"Unnumbered Sermons, Preached and Repreached between 1823-1876," ms.

The Way of Life. Philadelphia: American Sunday School Union, 1841.

"What is Christianity?" *Biblical Repertory and Princeton Review* 32, no. 1, 1860.

BENJAMIN B. WARFIELD

Apologetics or the Rational Vindication of Christianity, Francis R. Beattie, intro. by Benjamin B. Warfield. Richmond, Va.: Presbyterian Committee of Publications, 1903.

Biblical and Theological Studies. Philadelphia: Presbyterian and Reformed Publishing Company, 1952.

Calvin and Augustine. Philadelphia: The Presbyterian and Reformed Publishing Company, 1956.

The Divine Origin of the Bible. Philadelphia: Presbyterian Board of Publications, 1882.

"Drawing the Color Line." *The Independent*. July 5, 1888.

Faith and Life. New York: Longmans, Green, and Co., 1916.

Four Hymns and Some Religious Verses. Philadelphia: Westminster Press, 1910.

"The Gospel of the Incarnation." New York: Anson Randolph and Company, 1893.

Inaugural Address: The Idea of Systematic Theology, Considered as a Science. New York: Anson Randolph and Company, 1888.

"Inspiration." *Presbyterian Review,* 1881.

The Inspiration and Authority of the Bible. Philadelphia: Presbyterian and Reformed Publishing Company, 1964.

"The Latest Phase of Historical Rationalism." *Presbyterian Quarterly* 31, (1894).

" 'Miserable Sinner Christianity' in the Hands of the Rationalists." *Princeton Theological Review* 18 (1920).

Opuscula Warfieldii, collected works in 15 volumes.

Perfectionism. Philadelphia: Presbyterian and Reformed Publishing Company, 1967.

The Person and Work of Christ. Philadelphia: Presbyterian and Reformed Publishing Company, 1950.

The Power of God unto Salvation. Philadelphia: Presbyterian Board of Publication, 1903,

"The Religious Life of Theological Students." *Opuscula Warfieldii,* vol. 14.

"Review of *Mysticism,* Evelyn Underhill. . . ." *Princeton Theological Review* 12 (1914).

"Review of *Mysticism in Christianity,* W. K. Fleming. . . ." *Princeton Theological Review* 14 (1914).

"Review of *Mystik und geschichtliche Religion,* by Wilhelm Fresenius," *Princeton Theological Review* 12 (1914).

The Saviour of the World. New York: Hodder and Stoughton, 1913.

"Spiritual Culture in the Theological Seminary." *Opuscula Warfieldii,* vol. II.

Studies in Tertullian and Augustine. New York: Oxford University Press, 1930.

Studies in Theology. New York: Oxford University Press, 1932.

The Westminster Assembly and Its Work. New York: Oxford University Press, 1931.

Secondary Sources

Ahlstrom, Sydney E. "The Scottish Philosophy and American Theology." *Church History* 24 (1955).

Alexander, J. W. *The Life of Archibald Alexander*. New York: Charles Scribner, 1854.

Atlantic Monthly, "Johnson's Garrison and other Biographies," 47, (April, 1881).

Atwater, Lyman H. "A Discourse Commemorative of Dr. Charles Hodge." Princeton: Charles S. Robinson, 1878.

Calvin, John. *The Institutes of the Christian Religion,* ed. John T. McNeill. Philadelphia: The Westminster Press, 1960.

Cousar, R. W. "Benjamin B. Warfield: His Christology and Soteriology." Unpublished Ph.D. thesis, Edinburgh, 1954.

Dillenberger, John, and Claude Welch. *Protestant Christianity*. New York: Charles Scribner's Sons, 1954.

Dod, Albert B. "Finney's Lectures." *Biblical Repertory and Theological Review,* October, 1835.

Dowey, E. A. *The Knowledge of God in Calvin's Theology*. New York: Columbia University Press, 1952.

Gapp, Kenneth S. "The *Princeton Review* Series and the Contribution of Princeton Theological Seminary to Presbyterian Quarterly Magazines." Typescript, Princeton Theological Seminary, 1960.

Green, James B., ed. *A Harmony of the Westminster Presbyterian Standards*. Richmond: John Knox Press, 1965.

Hodge, Archibald Alexander. *The Life of Charles Hodge*. New York: Charles Scribner's Sons, 1880.

———. *Outlines of Theology*. New York: Robert Carter & Brothers, 1860.

"In Memoriam: Charles Hodge, Discourses Commemorative of the Life and Work of Charles Hodge." Henry B. Ashmead, Philadelphia, 1879.

Kennedy, Earl William. "Authors of Articles in the *Biblical Repertory and Princeton Review*." Typescript, Princeton Theological Seminary, 1963.

———. "Writings about Charles Hodge and His Works, Principally as Found in Periodicals Contained in the Speer Library, Princeton Theological Seminary for the Years 1830-1880." Typescript, Princeton Theological Seminary, 1963.

Kraus, Clyde Normon. "The Principle of Authority in the Theology of Benjamin B. Warfield, William Adams Brown, and Gerald Birney Smith." Unpublished Ph.D. thesis, Duke University, 1961.

Livingstone, William D. "The Princeton Apologetic as Exemplified by the Work of Benjamin B. Warfield and J. Gresham Machen: A Study in American Theology 1880-1930." Unpublished Ph.D. thesis, Yale, 1948.

Loetscher, Frederick Wm. "Archibald Alexander." *Dictionary of American Biography*, Allen Johnson, ed., vol. 1. New York: Charles Scribner's Sons, 1928.

Loetscher, Lefferts A. *The Broadening Church*. Philadelphia: University of Pennsylvania Press, 1954.

McAllister, James L., Jr. "The Nature of Religious Knowledge in the Theology of Charles Hodge." Unpublished Ph.D. thesis, Duke University, 1957.

Nelson, John O. "The Rise of the Princeton Theology." Unpublished Ph.D. thesis, Yale, 1935.

The New Englander, "Dr. Hodge's System of Theology," 117, no. 30, (1871).

Nichols, Robert H. "Benjamin B. Warfield." *Dictionary of American Biography*, Dumas Malone, ed., vol. 9, New York: Charles Scribner's Sons, 1936.

———. "Charles Hodge," *Dictionary of American Biography*, Dumas Malone, ed., vol. 9, New York: Charles Scribner's Sons, 1936.

Patton, Francis L. "Benjamin B. Warfield, A Memorial Address." *Princeton Theological Review* 19 (1921).

———. "Charles Hodge." *The Presbyterian Review* 2 (1881).

Pope, Earl A. "New England Calvinism and the Disruption in the Presbyterian Church." Unpublished Ph.D. thesis, Brown, 1962.

St. Amant, Penrose. "The Rise and Early Development of the Princeton School of Theology." Unpublished Ph.D. thesis, Edinburgh, 1952.

Salmond, C. A. *Princetonia: Charles and A. A. Hodge: with Class and Table Talk of Hodge the Younger.* London: Hamilton, Adams and Co., 1888.

Sandeen, Ernest R. "The Princeton Theology: One Source of Biblical Literalism in American Protestantism." *Church History* 31 (September, 1962).

———. "Toward a Historical Interpretation of the Origins of Fundamentalism." *Church History* 36 (March, 1967).

Schleiermacher, Friedrich. *The Christian Faith.* New York: Harper and Row Publishers, 1963.

Thorp, Willard, ed. *The Lives of Eighteen from Princeton.* Princeton: Princeton University Press, 1946.